Building a Workplace Writing Center

C000152638

This practical resource provides guidance for writing professionals to sustainably tackle the organizational writing challenges of any professional environment.

Rooted in applied experience, *Building a Workplace Writing Center* guides readers through the process of developing a writing center, from assessing the needs of an organization and pitching the idea of a writing center, to developing a service model and measuring progress. Chapters explore what a writing center can offer, such as one-on-one writing consultations, tailored group workshops, and standardized writing guidance and resources. Although establishing a writing center requires time and a shift in culture up front, it is a rewarding process that produces measurably improved writing, less frustration with the writing and revision processes, and more confident, independent writers.

This guide is an invaluable resource for professionals across industries and academia considering how to establish an embedded, sustainable, and cost-effective workplace writing center. It will be of particular interest to business and human resource managers considering how best to improve writing skills within their organizations.

Jessica Weber Metzenroth has helped establish workplace writing centers in both the US and Southeast Asia. She founded and directs the Writing Center at the Federal Reserve Bank of Philadelphia. She holds a PhD in Technical Communication and Rhetoric and has had her work and writings featured by *Harvard Business Review, WLN: A Journal of Writing Center Scholarship*, and the edited collection *How Stories Teach Us: Composition, Life Writing, and Blended Scholarship*.

Building a Workplace Writing Center

A Sustainable Solution and
Practical Guide

Jessica Weber Metzenroth

Routledge
Taylor & Francis Group

NEW YORK AND LONDON

Cover image: © ersinkisacik / Getty Images

First published 2022
by Routledge
605 Third Avenue, New York, NY 10158

and by Routledge
4 Park Square, Milton Park, Abingdon, Oxon, OX14 4RN

Routledge is an imprint of the Taylor & Francis Group, an informa business

© 2022 Jessica Weber Metzenroth

The right of Jessica Weber Metzenroth to be identified as author of this
work has been asserted in accordance with sections 77 and 78 of the
Copyright, Designs and Patents Act 1988.

All rights reserved. No part of this book may be reprinted or
reproduced or utilised in any form or by any electronic, mechanical,
or other means, now known or hereafter invented, including
photocopying and recording, or in any information storage or
retrieval system, without permission in writing from the publishers.

Trademark notice: Product or corporate names may be trademarks
or registered trademarks, and are used only for identification and
explanation without intent to infringe.

Library of Congress Cataloging-in-Publication Data
Names: Metzenroth, Jessica Weber, 1990– author.
Title: Building a workplace writing center : a sustainable solution and
practical guide / Jessica Weber Metzenroth.
Description: New York, NY : Routledge, 2022. |
Includes bibliographical references and index.
Identifiers: LCCN 2021049470 (print) | LCCN 2021049471 (ebook) |
ISBN 9781032081021 (hbk) | ISBN 9781032071077 (pbk) |
ISBN 9781003212959 (ebk)
Subjects: LCSH: Business writing. | Rhetoric—Study and teaching.
Classification: LCC HF5718.3 .M47 2022 (print) |
LCC HF5718.3 (ebook) | DDC 808.06/665—dc23/eng/20220110
LC record available at https://lccn.loc.gov/2021049470
LC ebook record available at https://lccn.loc.gov/2021049471

ISBN: 9781032081021 (hbk)
ISBN: 9781032071077 (pbk)
ISBN: 9781003212959 (ebk)

DOI: 10.4324/9781003212959

Typeset in Goudy
by codeMantra

Contents

PART 4
Workplace Writing Center Professional Development   121

Acknowledgments

Let me begin with deep gratitude for anyone who has ever trusted me to look at and talk about their writing, and for those who have done the same for me. This exchange of stories is some of the most important work I know.

For first trusting my instinct to start a writing center in a workplace, I'm immensely grateful for Eric Sonnheim and Joanne Branigan at the Federal Reserve Bank of Philadelphia. My fellow writing consultants past and present, Gayle Metzger and Chantel Gerardo, grew our little center to be so much more. The team at Bank Negara Malaysia also deserves my thanks for welcoming my ideas and supplying endless teh tarik, especially Alexa Yim, Jessica Chew, Christopher Lee Choon Keat, Kristina Rai, and Liyana @ Zanariah bt Ishak @ Bahari.

Because so much of this book evolved out of my dissertation for Texas Tech University's Technical Communication and Rhetoric program, I'd like to thank my advisor Dr. Ken Baake, and committee members Dr. Rebecca Rickly and Dr. Ted Roggenbuck. Dr. Ted deserves an extra thanks for nudging me toward writing center work when I was still an undergraduate at Bloomsburg University.

Enthusiastic cheers and gratitude to the TCR Fam, who know how to provide writing encouragement (and distractions) with just the right GIFs: Kristine Acosta, Delphine Jimenez Broccard, Manny Piña, Andrew Hollinger, and Kathleen Hardesty. Extra thanks to Dr. Kim Fain, who read over many proposals, shared her wisdom, and relayed her steadfast support.

The editorial team at Routledge, Brian Eschrich, Caroline Trussell, and Alyssa Turner provided immensely helpful support and guidance throughout the publishing process.

And of course, thanks to those who began and continuously feed my love for reading and writing. My parents, Ed and Lynn Weber, forced—I mean, nurtured—my writing abilities through many years of summer journals. Extra love to Jason Metzenroth, who cheered me on through every chapter, and to Juniper, who sweetly sleep-barked at my feet as I wrote this.

Introduction

Origin Stories

In my current role as a workplace writing center director, I frequently lead writing workshops with employees across the United States. I begin most of these workshops by asking participants to think about what they remember about learning to write as they grew up. Some participants share stories of teachers who had a positive impact on them, while some shudder as they recall diagramming sentences on a blackboard; in all cases, I encourage them to consider how this has shaped their attitudes toward and their confidence in their writing. It's an important part of their story, and it forms the basis of their learning...so it's only fair that I begin by sharing some of my earliest writing and writing center experiences, too. And I would encourage you to look back at your own path, which will inform the way the forthcoming chapters may resonate with you.

If you have picked up this book, it's likely because you are a "writing center person". Perhaps you are a peer or professional tutor, an academic writing center director, or simply someone who believes in the value of good writing and who has the patience to guide others toward it. But no matter the case, I'm willing to bet that you found your way into this work accidentally, as I suspect most of us do. I think that is partially why the question I am most frequently asked is: *How did you get into this work?*

Though more and more high schools and even some middle schools now boast their own writing centers, most people's first exposure to writing center work is in a college or university setting. I would find it hard to believe that anyone grows up imagining that one day they will become a writing center director or administrator. But perhaps the other primary driver toward writing center work is through gentle nudges (or sometimes, "voluntelling") by a mentor, colleague, or administrative authority.

In truth, I fall into this second category—through a series of nudges of varying force, I found myself drawn to this work. The first nudge was forceful: Every summer through fifth grade, my parents forced me to keep a journal, in alignment with our elementary school's recommendation. Most of the daily reminding, wheedling, begging, and threatening fell to my mom. The summer after fifth grade, she let me know that daily writing would no longer be

DOI: 10.4324/9781003212959-1

required. I immediately asked her if she could drive me to K-Mart to pick out a fresh notebook. I now hold a BA in Creative Writing; an MA in Composition, Language, and Rhetoric; and a PhD in Technical Communication and Rhetoric—my mom is convinced I earned each of these to spite her, and I can't say that wasn't just a *little* bit of it.

But I think the reason I hated journaling was because I was still learning to write, and it felt solitary (even with my mom's encouragement). I'd get a couple of stickers slapped on the front of my journal after I turned it in to a committee of teachers at the end of the summer, but that was it. I wasn't watching anyone else write, and my writing was only read to ensure completion. It wasn't until I grew curious about other writers at work and received thoughtful feedback that I cared about writing. I would hand essays to my mom and ask her to bust out a red pen before I turned them in to my teachers; slowly, the red began to dwindle. I would write down and staple together wild, scrap-paper stories for my rambunctious little brothers, grinning when they dissolved into helpless giggles. I entered a writing contest and won the best prize imaginable: a pass to feed the otters at a local zoo. And I once expelled all the bullies from a third-grade sleepover when I told a story so scary, they cried and called their parents to pick them up (my friends, of course, already knew all my stories). When I had a real audience in front of me, and I could get their feedback in constructive criticism, laughter, or surprise, I saw that writing gave me more power than anything else I could imagine.

What I came to love even more was the opportunity to help others with their writing. This began with informal requests to proofread my peers' essays in high school, but it morphed into something far beyond editing once I reached college. In my second semester at Bloomsburg University of Pennsylvania, I reached out to Dr. Ted Roggenbuck to ask for an interview to work in the on-campus Writing Center. As it turned out, interviews were typically only extended to students who had been nominated by a professor. I was a shy, quiet student, so my name had not yet come to his attention, but he graciously let me pick up an application anyway. Shortly thereafter, I enrolled in the upcoming fall semester's tutor training course. I was admittedly nervous to help students one-on-one, especially when I learned that I would be working with more senior (and sometimes even graduate) students on a fairly regular basis. But as the semester progressed, I learned names like *Bruffee, Lunsford, Eodice*, and felt well-enough equipped to apply theory more and more to my tutoring sessions. As many novice tutors do, I found myself paying less attention to grammatical mistakes, and paying more attention to helping writers tell their stories clearly and effectively.

I quickly struck up a relationship with two students in particular: two exchange students from Russia who referred to themselves simply as *The Olgas*, as they had frequently mispronounced last names, had the same first name, and spent almost all of their time together. I don't remember if The Olgas first came to the writing center for a joint session or if one referred the other after working with me, but they began to frequent the writing center and ask for me by name. Being able to help guide them through papers written in their second language was a challenge but a pleasure—learning from them in exchange was an unexpected joy. To thank me for my help in the writing center, they invited me to dinner one night at their upper-campus apartment. A friend and I arrived to an unbelievable spread of their favorite recipes from home: salmon topped with slices of bright lemon, cradled in cream-puddled tin foil packets; dark, rich borscht; crisp salads with glittering pomegranate arils. We stayed so late talking about the differences between our home countries and eating plate after plate that we almost missed the last shuttle bus back to our lower-campus dorms. I continued to work with The Olgas periodically until they returned to Russia, and we kept up regular dinners together.

From that point, my tutoring style became more collaborative, more focused on mutual development. I started to listen to the stories that students brought to me, and I tried my best to help them tell their stories in a way that did them justice. I started to ask as many questions as they did. Some students arrived skeptical or frustrated; some students cried about pending due dates or confronting the overly personal topic they'd chosen. But my mission was always to have at least one point of connection, one laugh, or one helpful suggestion in the course of a tutoring session. Most of the time, my tutees and I would manage just that.

I don't think that my early exposure to the world of writing centers was particularly unique. Drop in to any writing center-related conference, and you're likely to hear about innovative tutoring approaches, surprising tutor–tutee bonds, and a shift in focus from lower-order concerns to higher-order concerns. And my involvement with writing centers may have ended there, as it often does when peer tutors graduate, if not for a kind but forceful nudge from the same Dr. Roggenbuck who first hired me as a tutor. Although I had already been accepted to a graduate program in Curriculum & Instruction—with the goal of becoming a high school English teacher—Dr. R encouraged me to instead apply for a graduate assistantship at Salisbury University and to study Composition and Rhetoric, a popular track for writing center work. I had never heard of Salisbury University, and I had only recently been able to define *rhetoric* succinctly. But, knowing his audience, Dr. R made two arguments that were too compelling for me to refuse: the graduate assistantship was a position as the assistant director of the campus writing center, and the campus itself was only a 25-minute drive from the beach.

So, I reversed course. I applied for and accepted the assistant director position. I loved the work. And I drove to the beach as often as the weather would allow.

While serving as the assistant director of Salisbury University's writing center, I helped train a diverse staff of undergraduate tutors. I also continued to fill in with some tutoring sessions, especially when graduate students at satellite campuses called in to work with a tutor remotely. By the time I completed my Masters, I had decided not to apply to PhD programs. A professor had shown us the slim list of job postings for English professors across the country, especially in the wake of the recession. I was ready to return to the Philadelphia area, in part to be closer to family and friends. I was hopeful that my work could still involve working with students on their writing skills—if I had to, I could always enter a certificate program for teaching. So, I moved back home and spent a blisteringly hot summer applying to jobs in every semi-related market I could think of.

I had been offered two different full-time jobs by that September. The trouble was that I hadn't gotten either offer in writing before I started looking at apartments in Philadelphia. The first job offer was as a content creator for a company that produced educational testing materials; this company told me for so many weeks that "HR was working on the offer paperwork" that I started my job search over. As I write this seven years later, I think that paperwork may still actually be sitting with HR—they never gave me any other updates. The second offer was a secretarial position at a tutoring company, with the promise that I could work my way into more tutoring-related or tutor manager-related positions that may become available. I took this job over the phone on a Friday, signed an apartment lease on that Saturday, and received a call back from the company on Monday that said, on second thought, they had decided I was overqualified and that I didn't need to come into the office and sign the paperwork, after all.

Cue life crisis.

It was at this time that my mom ran into a family friend at a Labor Day picnic. The friend was talking about how his department was thinking through ways to better support staff writing skills. "Oh!" my mom jumped at this excitedly, "My daughter could help with that!" She returned from the picnic with two goodies for me: a patriotically frosted cupcake and this story of her mortifying push for my employment. But the friend had promised to let us know when an anticipated job opening was posted, and, a few weeks later, he sent the link along.

The job posted was for an *Examination Report Review Analyst II* at the Federal Reserve Bank of Philadelphia,[1] which is the last position I ever could have imagined myself applying for. The job description was vague, but it did seem to involve some kind of editorial or writing-related work, so I submitted my resume, and the friend promised to put in a good word.

Here are some of the lessons that I learned as a writing center tutor, and again as an assistant director: *Ask questions. Be honest when you don't know something. It's okay to request a moment to think or to pause to look something up. Figure out clients' goals and interests. Negotiate meaning together, but let them lead. Bounce ideas around to see what sticks. Leave the session with them feeling better about the work than they did when they started.* I pulled all of these lessons out in my interview.

I had the good fortune of having three incredibly open-minded, patient leaders on my interview panel. Our discussion lasted nearly two hours, but a defining moment was when I asked if they had ever considered having an in-house trainer who could provide ongoing, one-on-one support to writers;

I suggested that this would be more sustainable than bringing in an expert to lead workshops from time to time, as they'd been doing. More than fixing any issues at the source, I argued that a writing center model could help improve staff's confidence, ease managers' frustrations, and provide sustainable writing improvement. I shared stories of the two high school writing centers that I had helped found: one with a colleague while I was an undergraduate, and one independently as a graduate student.

But then the panel asked me what other workplace writing center models we could look to, at which point I sheepishly admitted, "Oh…I don't think there *are* any".

My dad called me after the interview to ask how it went. "Great", I answered, percolating with excitement, "We talked about writing centers most of the time"! I heard my dad sigh on the other end, preparing to remind me that *this was not a writing center job interview.* I pictured him motioning to my mom to stop rolling her yoga equipment into the bedroom that had been relinquished by their first to leave the nest, suspecting this arrangement might be temporary.

I remember eating two scoops of gelato for lunch after my interview, sitting at an outdoor table on Passyunk and sketching out what a workplace writing center might look like. Though I had spent years helping students of all ages learn to communicate more effectively, I began to realize how valuable this support could be for professionals—even those with long-standing careers. These conversations between "writing center people" and most nonacademic workplaces had just not happened yet.

Two weeks later, I was offered the job. They even let me use a different informal title: *writing consultant.* And though our one-woman writing center team has since expanded, and we've even helped replicate a workplace writing center in Kuala Lumpur, this is still new ground.

But that's where you come in. Perhaps this guide can help you to identify and/or approach a professional space that could benefit from a writing center. Perhaps it can help you envision a career path you didn't know was possible before. Perhaps it can help you to create shifts in your organization that encourage people to communicate more clearly and to be open to improvement. In any case, I still recommend the gelato first.

Jessica Weber Metzenroth
South Philadelphia

March 2021

Note

1 The views expressed in this book do not necessarily reflect the views of the Federal Reserve Bank of Philadelphia or of the Federal Reserve System.

Part 1

Welcome to the Writing Center

1   Throwing Open the Doors

The writing center at the Federal Reserve Bank of Philadelphia[1] began as just a small office. Aside from my corner desk, the office contained just a small table with two chairs and a large whiteboard centered above. Each morning, I'd set down my coffee and update the whiteboard with two items: the date, and a word of the day. I kept the door open as often as possible, so people passing by would feel more comfortable entering to borrow a book or to ask me a question. In the early days, most people probably poked their heads in to puzzle over why I was there; gradually, a few people made it part of their morning routine to see the word of the day.

As I've done each morning in the office, I'll start with some definitions. Following are key words and phrases explained within the context of this book.

Key Words and Phrases

Writing Center

Though I'll dive into more about the history of writing centers in the following chapter, let's start with a basic overview. Though traditionally found in academic environments, a *writing center* involves the one-to-one teaching of writing. Writing center mission statements are often informed by North's famed axiom: "we aim to make better writers, not necessarily—or immediately—better texts" (1984, p. 441). Learning is meant to be collaborative, at a peer level, organic and yet intersectional (Bruffee, 1984). As Muriel Harris points out, writing centers should welcome students working on all types of writing assignments, "at all levels of writing proficiency" (2006). But beyond those general guidelines, there is no one model for a writing center. Eric Hobson writes that "each program has a distinct personality; each center is defined as much by its local context as by any overarching definition of 'writing center'" (2001, p. 169).

Though I will touch on my own experiences throughout this book, I will refer to workplace writing centers more broadly as a concept that

DOI: 10.4324/9781003212959-3

can be applied in any nonacademic environment. The workplace writing center should be understood as a separate resource from traditional editorial staff (e.g., those situated in public affairs or internal communications). It is a space created with the intention of coaching writers through improving their own written pieces, with the ultimate goal of building sustainable writing skills among staff. Writers' development, not public-facing perfection, is the goal.

When referring to my own experience, I'm apt to use the phrase *our writing center*. The writing centers that I've helped establish and have directed have always involved far more people beyond me. And as I've worked to launch writing centers in academic and nonacademic spaces, I've paid particular mind to ensuring a sustainable model that will last beyond my hands-on help.

Workplace

Workplace will be used to mean any professional environment in which you might consider building a writing center. This may include a corporation, a government organization, a nonprofit entity, and so on.

Though I acknowledge and respect academic spaces as workplaces that employ many professionals, they will be excluded from this *workplace* category. Many colleges and universities have existing writing centers, and academic writing center models are well established. It is not uncommon for academic writing centers to even extend their services to faculty and staff. But nonacademic workplaces face unique challenges and benefits when creating a writing center. The relationships between writers, consultants, and authorities are different from those found in traditional writing centers, and the embeddedness of the model differs.

Writer

Writer will refer to an employee at any level who completes written tasks as a part of their job function. They are the potential clients and targeted audience of the writing center, whether or not they choose to use it. The writing they bring to the writing center will vary widely depending on the workplace itself: e.g., memos, emails, formal reports, proposals, white papers, articles, social media posts, briefings, and presentation slides.

Consultant

I will use *consultant* to refer to employees working within a workplace writing center. Different workplaces use varying titles and tiers to refer to employees; in some environments, formal titles may look more like analyst, subject matter expert, director, manager. But for the purposes of this book, understand *consultant* to mean an employee who supports the work of the writing center, primarily by providing one-on-one writing consultations.

Consultation

Consultation will refer to a collaborative meeting between a writer and a writing center consultant. Though workplace writing centers can offer a variety of services (see Chapter 5), the signature offering is a one-on-one [or group] consultation. *Writing center session* may be used interchangeably with *consultation*.

The language that we use when referring to writing center spaces, services, and staff are important; such language will also vary depending on the needs of each individual workplace. This will be further explored in Chapter 6.

A Day in the Life of a Workplace Writing Center Director

First things first: Unlock the door to the Writing Center, turn on the lights, and update the date and word of the day on the whiteboard. I prop the door open so that anyone passing by will feel welcome to stop in.

I check our online scheduler and see that a writer has booked an afternoon video appointment with one of our consultants. The consultant, Gayle, is working remotely today but is already immersed in a report that the writer submitted in advance. Gayle takes notes and prepares for the session, checking back at our record log to remember what she and the writer have worked on together before.

Around 10 AM, an HR representative is walking around with a new hire, introducing him to resources in the department. I greet the new hire, explain the Writing Center's services and how we can be of help as he settles into his new role. I give him a copy of our spiral-bound *Writing Guide*, some branded pens, and my business card, inviting him to reach out sometime so we can show him how to schedule a consultation.

At 11 AM, another consultant, Chantel, sends me a slide deck for an upcoming workshop. She has developed an hour's worth of instruction to address writing challenges that a special team in our department has been dealing with. Over the past few weeks, she's worked closely with the team's manager to determine what hands-on activities and examples will help participants to absorb and retain the instruction.

As I'm eating my lunch, a writer knocks on the open door to ask if we have any resources for drafting succinct meeting notes. I take a moment to show her an online video module that we've created on our intranet site, and I also pull a few books from the shelves behind my desk. I invite her to sit at the consultation table and page through them. She helps herself to some sticky notes, marking helpful pages to photocopy, and she asks to borrow one of the books through the end of the week.

At 2 PM, Chantel pulls up a chair at my desk, and we hop onto a conference call with Gayle. For the next 45 minutes, we'll be talking through a stack of applications that have come in for the Writing Center's summer internship position. We'll also take some time to bounce around ideas for a proposal to submit to a regional conference.

By 4 PM, I am wrapping up a brief article for our workplace's internal newsletter. Our Writing Center recently completed a milestone number of consultations, and I want to share this accomplishment with other employees—not just to highlight the work that our team is doing, but to remind readers that we are a widely used resource that is available every day.

Just before I leave for the day, Gayle calls me to talk through some resistance she faced from the writer in the afternoon's consultation. We talk about what strategies she used, and how we can tactfully document the resistance.

Asking me to describe a typical day in our Writing Center is one of the questions I'm most frequently asked by those interested in starting their own workplace writing centers. In truth, every day is completely different. When a major report is coming due in the department, we may have a flood of session requests to go through different sections of the report with individual writers. Over the summer, we may experience a lull of session requests as writers use up vacation time; then, we can pivot our services to updating our print and online resources with the help of a paid intern. We are constantly reconsidering the ways in which we meet our workplace's needs, as the needs are always changing. We check in frequently with the writers we serve, in order to get their honest feedback, and we ask department leaders to share how we can help our colleagues meet high-priority objectives.

Leading a workplace writing center has allowed me to be creative, analytical, and constantly challenged every day. It is certainly an opportunity that may appeal to those who have had writing center experience in an academic realm. And because many universities and colleges employ only one full-time director [or a limited number of professional tutors], the addition of writing centers in the workplace could mean more career opportunities in a wider variety of geographic and industry settings. I also find myself navigating less stressful relationships with employers than do many of my colleagues employed by academic institutions.

Attractive Alternative to Academic Work

Many writing center professionals and administrators find themselves in frustrating or precarious positions within their universities. Across the field, writing

center positions display a huge variance in status, ranging from a level equivalent with a secretary to a level equivalent to a vice provost (Geller & Denny,
2013, p. 100). And yet, Geller and Denny found that "[i]nstitutional status actually appears to have an inverse relationship with individual satisfaction" (p.
103). Writing center professionals who enjoyed higher status reported feeling
more pressure from their institutions. Those who were acknowledged at a lower
level struggled with a commonly reported complaint in this field: their intel-
lectual work and administrative duties were invisible or undervalued (p. 117).

Another challenge that writing center professionals face in academic environments is the typical expectation that they must manage *every* aspect of
the writing center. Writing center professionals tend to find themselves involved with "accounting, budgeting, human resources performance appraisals,
the logistics of hiring and payroll, and the mechanics of prepping, educating,
and monitoring staff" (Geller & Denny, 2013, p. 110). And yet, despite these
efforts, they also find themselves lacking a clear path to advancement and
recognition (p. 105). Because our workplace writing center has been embedded
within an established department, we have avoided some of these pitfalls. We
have access to other supporting units who handle accounting and budgeting,
as well as who assist us with hiring processes. This support allows us to focus on
helping writers, networking with our field, and measuring our progress. As our
writing center has become more established over the past several years, we've
been able to work with human resources specialists and department leadership
to map out career trajectories and paths for advancement. Their assistance, as
well as other department units to follow as a model, is immeasurably helpful.

Another common complaint from writing center professionals working in
academic environments is that budgets are extremely limited or are inconsis-
tent (Perdue & Driscoll, 2017). Some writing center directors find themselves
unable to pay the student consultants they employ, or spend a great deal of
time fighting for their compensation. Although our writing center needs to be
budget conscious and is working within bounds set by others within our department (and the workplace as a whole), we have so far been supported in all
of our research and professional development goals. Gratefully, my workplace
recognizes the value in sharing research, as well as in committing to ongoing
training and networking with professional organizations. I would imagine that
any writing centers established in more corporate settings may find themselves
with even more liberal budgets than we have. In either case, my professional
development activities feel far less burdensome than they did when I was the
assistant director of a university writing center. Within my university, I remember having to complete 500-word essays every time I wanted to attend a
conference and receive some funding to offset the cost—even if the conference was close enough to avoid purchasing airfare. I am prudent with resources
in professional spaces, and of course there is still paperwork involved, but I
have never been asked to self-fund these important opportunities or to com-
pose an essay justifying my request. In general, a workplace willing to invest in
a workplace writing center is likely to be equally supportive of ongoing professional development opportunities for writing center staff.

Perhaps the most frustrating challenge that writing center professionals in academic environments face is the way in which their environment "ignore[s] their expertise" and "challenge[s] their status as educators" (Perdue & Driscoll, 2017, p. 203). Although I have had some minor conflicts with individuals, I have been treated like a professional and an expert in my field within my workplace as a whole. Whereas my colleagues who work in academia have expressed feeling pressure to constantly prove themselves with publications, I was hired because my workplace already saw me as a capable professional. The reason they've invested in our team is because they trust us to provide the service we promised. Though every organization will be different, I think many workplaces are likely to offer an environment that would allow writing center professionals to pursue the research, projects, and methods they think are best.

One particularly interesting account that I've come across is Dyke Ford's "Going Rogue: How I Became a Communication Specialist in an Engineering Department" (2018). This piece resonated because Dyke Ford similarly found herself as the only communication specialist within a highly technical field that was at first unfamiliar to her. Though the prospect of working within an unfamiliar environment is daunting for just about anyone, Dyke Ford notes many of the advantages that I have enjoyed in my own role. Some of the benefits include "research collaboration opportunities" with other professionals, "funding opportunities", "lower course loads", "increased salary rate", and "greater opportunities to witness students' evolution of skills" (p. 340). Although some might assume that a communication specialist in an engineering (or other similarly technical) department may be ignored, the opposite effect seems to be true: They are valued as a resource that was previously unavailable. Dyke Ford's nod to salary and funding reflect my experience in transitioning from working in an academic writing center as an assistant director to directing a workplace writing center. Portions of this very book are the result of collaboration with experts in other fields, so I can personally vouch for the exciting opportunities that can come from working with experts in other disciplines. One of the most alluring items on this list may, for members of academia, be "lower course loads". Whereas writing center directors frequently find themselves taking on additional courses in addition to their writing center work, I have never been tasked with this. All of our writing center consultants are able to offer workshops when it makes sense for our schedule and for the writers' schedules. Some months are busier than others, but we've had full control over what workshops we plan to teach and how long we need to prepare for them. This freedom alone would alleviate much of the stress placed on writing center professionals. As for me, one of Dyke Ford's most compelling points is the ability to see individuals develop. As the only communications specialist in her department, anyone needing communications help was sent to her; it is similar within our writing center. We have the ability to work with the same people many times over the course of our careers. Whereas writing center directors typically must adapt to seeing their students or tutors turn over every year or every four years, a workplace writing center director can develop longer-lasting relationships with department members. Just last year, I attended a retirement ceremony for a man that I (and other writing center consultants) had worked with since our very first few months on the job. When we released the first edition of our little *Writing Guide*, he kept it in his shirt pocket to reference for several weeks. His cubicle was a few rows over from the writing center, and for years we heard about how his children were doing, what emails were troubling him, how he felt he was improving in his writing. Those are the moments that have made me love my job most, and that I know would appeal to many writing center professionals.

Workplace Interest and Expected Benefits

Another question that writing center professionals frequently ask: *How do you convince a workplace that they need to improve their writing?* I would argue that it probably wouldn't take much convincing! Workplaces typically know the value of good writing skills, and there is no shortage of research on this topic.

Value of Effective Employee Writing

Employers consistently rank writing and communication skills as a top requirement for applicants (Gray, Emerson, & MacKay, 2005; Marcel, 2017; Spartz & Weber, 2015). And though many people mistakenly believe that technology has decreased our need for writing skills, in fact "the demand for strong written skills is growing, not decreasing, with developing technologies... and the ever-intensifying focus on the bottom line" (Gray et al., 2005, p. 430). Poor writing skills can be incredibly time-consuming and costly for organizations. Some estimates place the cost of unclear writing at around $400 billion annually (Bernoff, 2017b). The United States private sector alone spends $3.1 billion annually to provide some kind of writing training for employees (Gray et al., 2005, p. 433).

Inspiring Writer Motivation and Confidence

Workplace writing centers provide an immediate reader that can respond to a writer's impact. Consultants can help express the reader's goals and needs, pointing out where the writer's "language shuts out readers" (Garwood, 2013, p. 176). When we can shift our observations to those of an envisioned reader, we can also employ "politeness strategies to soften face-threatening speech acts" (Mackiewicz, 2011, p. 445). As writing consultants with dedicated time for coaching writers through revision, we can motivate our colleagues with praise, empathy, and, at times, hedging. We can also encourage writers toward intrinsic motivation by "providing a writer with direction for where to go next, helping a writer improve his or her writing process, and showing the writer that his or her project is meaningful and interesting" (DeCheck, 2012, p. 35). In addition to providing individualized feedback, writing center consultants can also help manage collaborative writing and revision (Colen & Petelin, 2004).

Not only can investing in writers' skills increase independence and productivity, it can also foster motivation (Stowers & Barker, 2010, p. 365). Traditional feedback tends to focus on correcting mistakes, which can decrease writers' confidence; one way to counteract this is to use workshopping and coaching methods that provide ongoing feedback and expose writers to the work of others (Mascle, 2013). This can also aid in the important work of helping "beginning workers understand their economic relationship to institutional and economic discourses and how they can shape these discourses" (Wilson & Wolford, 2017, p. 25). We know that each industry has its own way of communicating, but we often overlook the fact that each workplace can have its own dialect within an industry. The more we are able to help writers understand communication expectations clearly, the more we can help raise their self-efficacy (Housley Gaffney, 2014, p. 176).

Overview

So far, we have established key terms for workplace writing centers. We've peeked into the daily operations of an existing workplace writing center. And now we have established, at least cursorily, that there are a variety of reasons why both writing center professionals and workplaces would be interested in forging workplace writing centers.

Before we can look too far into the future of workplace writing centers, it's important to take a look at the past; the next chapter will provide a brief history of writing centers. It will also begin to explore traditional writing support methods and services currently used in professional industries, as well as why workplace writing centers are a more sustainable solution. Workplaces are evolving at an ever-quickening pace, and the time has never been better to help writers in all contexts adapt and thrive.

The following section of this book, *Building the Writing Center*, will provide an overview of what needs to be in place for a successful writing center. This includes tips on gaining management's support and paving the way for long-term success. Chapters 3 and 4 will help you to create the earliest blueprints for your workplace writing center, from setting reasonable expectations to mapping out the relationships and dynamics of your workplace. Chapters 5 and 6 will help you to further shape the vision you have for your workplace writing center. Practical guidance will lead you through determining what services your center will offer, as well as setting a mission statement, developing branding strategies, and launching marketing campaigns.

The third section of this book, *Measuring and Communicating Progress*, will help you to consider the ways in which you can track the writing center's progress in a way that is valuable to your workplace. Chapter 7 dives into needs assessments and ways that you can establish baseline measures of writing performance and challenges. Chapter 8 provides an overview of data logs, and how you can maintain records that protect your center as well as the writers who use it. Chapters 9 and 10 explore ways that you can use data to show your writing center's impact, including through surveys and pretest/posttest quasi-experiment.

The concluding section of this book, *Workplace Writing Center Professional Development*, will propose ways that you [and/or your staff] can grow within and beyond your workplace writing center. Shifting from an academic to a workplace writing center presents some challenges, which will be explored in Chapter 11. Chapter 12 provides further insight into education and experience to consider when recruiting individuals to work in a workplace writing center; it also suggests ways to build on this knowledge even further through professional development opportunities. Chapter 13 considers ways that you can harness your workplace writing center's powers for good, by giving back to your community and even helping other writing centers to launch.

By the time you reach the conclusion in Chapter 14, I hope that you will feel confident in your own journey to create a workplace writing center. And I encourage you to reach out with stories of your successes so that we can grow this new community together.

Note

1 The writing center at the Federal Reserve Bank of Philadelphia is the first one that I have established in a workplace. Since then, I have helped another central bank set up a writing center, and I have also advised many more people on how they can create writing centers within their own workplaces. The experiences I share in this book come from founding and leading writing centers in high schools, universities, and workplaces—not solely or specifically from my time at the Federal Reserve.

References

Bernoff, J. (2017, April 13). Bad writing costs businesses billions. *The Daily Beast*. Retrieved from https://www.thedailybeast.com/bad-writing-costs-businesses-billions.

Bruffee, K. (1984). Collaborative learning and the "conversation of mankind". *College English*, 46(7), 635–652. https://doi.org/10.2307/376924.

Colen, K., & Petelin, R. (2004). Challenges in collaborative writing in the contemporary corporation. *Corporate Communications*, 9(2), 136–145.

DeCheck, N. (2012). The power of common interest for motivating writers: A case study. *Writing Center Journal*, 32(1), 28–38.

Dyke Ford, J. (2018). Going rogue: How I became a communication specialist in an engineering department. *Technical Communication Quarterly*, 27(4), 336–342, https://doi.org/10.1080/10572252.2018.1518511

Garwood, K. (2013). Metonymy and plain language. *Journal of Technical Writing & Communication*, 43(2), 165–180. https://doi-org.lib-e2.lib.ttu.edu/10.2190/TW.43.2.d

Geller, A. E., & Denny, H. (2013). Of ladybugs, low status, and loving the job: Writing center professionals navigating their careers. *Writing Center Journal*, 33(1), 96–129.

Gray, F. E., Emerson, L., & MacKay, B. (2005, December). Meeting the demands of the workplace: Science students and written skills. *Journal of Science Education and Technology*, 14(4). Retrieved from https://www.jstor.org/stable/40186675.

Harris, M. (2006). The concept of a writing center. Retrieved from http://writingcenters. org/writing-center-concept-by-muriel-harris/.

Hobson, E. (2001). Writing center pedagogy. In G. Tate, A. Rupiper, & K. Schick (Eds.), *A Guide to Composition Pedagogies* (pp. 165–182). New York: Oxford University Press.

Housley Gaffney, A. L. (2014). Communication instruction in landscape architecture courses: A model and effects on students' self-efficacy. *Journal of Business and Technical Communication, 28*(2), 158–186. https://doi.org/10.1177/1050651913513903

Mackiewicz, J. (2011). Epinions advisors as technical editors: Using politeness across levels of edit. *Journal of Business and Technical Communication, 25*(4), 421–448. https://doi.org/10.1177/1050651911411038

Marcel, M. (2017). User feedback: Alumni on workplace presenting and improving courses. *Business and Professional Communication Quarterly, 80*(4), 484–515. https:// doi.org/10.1177/2329490617695895

Mascle, D. D. (2013). Writing self-efficacy and written communication skills. *Business Communication Quarterly, 76*(2), 216–225. https://doi.org/10.1177/1080569913480234

North, S. M. (1984, September). The idea of a writing center. *College English, 46*(5), 433–446.

Perdue, S. W., & Driscoll, D. L. (2017). Context matters: Centering writing center administrators' institutional status and scholarly identity. *Writing Center Journal, 36*(1), 185–214.

Spartz, J. M., & Weber, R. P. (2015). Writing entrepreneurs: A survey of attitudes, habits, skills, and genres. *Journal of Business and Technical Communication, 29*(4), 428–455. https://doi.org/10.1177/1050651915588145

Stowers, R. H., & Barker, R. T. (2010). The coaching and mentoring process: The obvious knowledge and skill set for organizational communication professors. *Journal of Technical Writing & Communication, 40*(3), 363–371. https://doi-org.lib-e2.lib.ttu. edu/10.2190/TW.40.3.g

Wilson, G., & Wolford, R. (2017). The technical communicator as (post-postmodern) discourse worker. *Journal of Business and Technical Communication, 31*(1), 3–29. https://doi.org/10.1177/1050651916667531

2 A Look Back at Writing Center History and a Look Ahead to New Frontiers

History of Writing Centers: Meet People Where They Are

In the last several decades, writing centers have enjoyed a rise in visibility in the university as well as within a growing field of scholarship. But writing centers, in one form or another, long predate this trend. Some of the earliest recognized writing center prototypes were writing "laboratories", including one at a St. Louis high school in 1904 (Carino, 1995, p. 105). Throughout the twentieth century, drastic shifts in the political environment shaped the American education system and the students enrolled; writing centers emerged and responded with these waves. After mass education initiatives in the 1930s, the University of Minnesota created a course-bound writing lab to help underprepared students, while the State University of Iowa "established separate facilities for laboratory instruction"—a monumental moment in writing centers carving out their own space (Carino, 1995, p. 106). Throughout the 1940s, more free-standing models were born, largely in response to the emphasis on military communication during World War II. Though the 1950s saw a dip in writing center scholarship, possibly due to the increased emphasis on math and science in the wake of the Space Race (Berlin, 1987, p. 121), writing centers again began to flourish in the 1960s after open admissions policies welcomed in the "most diverse group ever of rising adults" (Carino, 1996, p. 32). And in about a decade, the writing center community formed its channels of scholarship, exchanging ideas in publications like *Writing Lab Newsletter*, established in 1977; the *Writing Center Journal*, established in 1980; and at functions hosted by the International Writing Centers Association (IWCA), founded in 1983. Prior to these outlets, it was common for writing center directors to feel isolated in their roles, unsure of best practices. Muriel Harris, *Writing Lab Newsletter*'s founder, wrote years later that first-time directors often felt "we were playing a violin while constructing it" (1997, p. 136).

Even as I first dove into the world of academic writing centers as an undergraduate tutor, I was excited by the ways the field was breaking new ground. Writing centers were returning to high schools with the guidance of scholars like Richard Kent (2006) and affiliations like the Secondary School Writing Centers Association, founded in 2010. Bloomsburg University's tutor training, where I had my own first exposure to the world of writing centers, included

DOI: 10.4324/9781003212959-4

weeks focused on digital literacies and how to move beyond pen-and-paper sessions in order to reach off-campus and nontraditional students. As student bodies become even more diverse and writing center scholars think even more creatively, we continue to see the writing center world expand in promising new directions.

The spaces we create, whether established in basements or libraries or on-line, are meant to be safe spaces, though we must also address the tensions that can arise (Geller, Eodice, Condon, Carroll, & Boquet, 2007, p. 7). Despite the strides made over the last century, writing centers and their administrators face a number of challenges. One common misconception is that writing centers are remedial spaces, often "defined by external curriculum" (North, 1984, p. 440). Ede posited that writing centers are seen as "pedagogical fix-it shops", in part because writing is traditionally seen as a solitary activity (1989, p. 7). Historically, it seems that interest in and funding for writing centers spike after a new population of underprepared students arrives at the university. We identify a problem—that students are struggling to write—and we prescribe a solution: The writing center will fix them. I would be remiss not to acknowledge that the workplace writing centers I've helped start were also funded in response to such a perceived gap, albeit in professionals' writing skills. This challenge is particularly problematic for a number of reasons. First and foremost, the writing center's services become stigmatized when others assume that we are here only to treat or diagnose struggling writers. It also places pressure on writing center administrators (WCAs) to account for measurable improvement in students' grades, proficiency, or retention. Though proof of effectiveness is not necessarily a bad thing, it detracts from the vital work that comes from everyday conversations and unseen strides that tutors (or consultants) and writers make together.

Additionally, WCAs already have a long and exhausting history of fighting for success and recognition. While a writing center may serve hundreds or even thousands of students in a semester, they are often led by a solitary director and a staff of students who need to be recruited and trained in new batches *every academic year.* And though writing center models vary, the professional standing of WCAs varies even more wildly. Depending on the institution, some WCAs "are classified at levels similar to administrative or secretarial positions while others may be at the level of a vice provost or dean" (Geller & Denny, 2013, p. 100). Perdue and Driscoll's 2017 study proved that "many WCAs work within environments that ignore their expertise, challenge their status as educators, discourage their research, and under-resource them to boot" (p. 203). This position is even more precarious for WCAs of minority status; additional pushback can arise in the face of their gender, race, orientation, or ethnicity (Ore, 2017).

These challenges aren't new, and WCAs have proposed and pursued a number of solutions. One idea is to create and/or enforce a system of standard accreditation. But as of 2017, "87.2% of [surveyed] centers were not certified through existing organizations", even though 52.5% of centers had explored the idea (Carpenter, Whiddon, & Morin, 2017, p. 5). Some of the reasons given for not pursuing accreditation included difficulty of contacting the certifying entity, expensive fees, labor intensity, and inappropriate requirements. Beyond these hurdles, other writing center scholars have raised concerns about how our work may be compromised if we pursue professionalism too aggressively. This pursuit extends beyond systems of standardized accreditation, or even regional accreditation, as Carpenter et al. suggest (2017). In 1994, Riley warned the field that if we professionalized in the traditions of other English-related disciplines (e.g., literature, composition) we could "end up recreating most of the debilitating hierarchies that we wished to escape", trading "collaboration, spontaneity, freedom, equality, courage", for "constructions of expert and amateur, of protocol, instruction, and tradition" (p. 31). Riley recognized that our subversive practices can contribute to our marginalization—but he also pointed out that this subversive nature is at our very core. Trimbur identified another conundrum in 1989: Namely, that if we focus too much on collaboration, we risk homogenizing diverse voices. Many writing tutors and directors, similarly, navigate the paradoxical nature of writing consultations: *Work alongside and with the writer, but make sure the product reflects the writer's voice.* Trimbur suggests managing these challenges by focusing on conversation rather than consensus; but, again, the major issue with accreditation as a possibility right now is that there *is* no consensus. These authors share an underlying anxiety about whether approaching the very system that may earn us recognition will also signal the end of the work we do.

Meanwhile, in recent years, Lerner has pointed to a fear of *underwhelming* collaboration between writing center scholars. In his analysis of the *Writing Center Journal*, he problematizes the fact that it "has by and large featured single-authored articles despite an ethos of collaborative work" (2014, p. 68). So not only are WCAs receiving mixed messages from their institutions about whether or not their research is important, they now also face criticism that existing research is not collaborative enough within or beyond the discipline.

The writing center discipline, despite being relatively young, has grown enough to face the existential crises that other English disciplines know all too well. So, in the midst of this confusion and division, why, exactly, would I argue that we should bring writing centers into an entirely new realm? Because, as I've seen firsthand, it can introduce new opportunities to the field, as well as a valuable resource in the workplaces served. Rather than becoming too insular and status-focused, perhaps new writing centers could be introduced to the workplace as a return to the collaborative, interdisciplinary, subversive work where we began. We can get our hands muddy again.

Since I began the workplace writing center at the Federal Reserve Bank of Philadelphia, I've heard from a number of writing center tutors and directors who are interested in following a similar career path. In my own position, I've since been able to hire two different writing consultants to help staff our center, as well as hire five paid undergraduate interns, one each in consecutive summers. Though I only have my own experience to share, I can see that writing centers in workplace environments are relieved of some of the burdens placed on academic writing centers. My team members and I have enjoyed stable jobs with excellent benefits and opportunities for advancement; as full-time employees, we have not had to worry about budget cuts or ensuring tenure. We are able to focus on producing and sharing our research, as our workplace recognizes the visibility that comes from innovative thinking and producing results. We have also been able to ensure funding for conferences and external training with little resistance, as the Federal Reserve Bank of Philadelphia is an academy company that values ongoing training and development. For those in underfunded or undervalued writing centers, I know our jobs can sound too good to be true. This isn't to say that all workplace writing centers will find the same institutional support as ours has—each will face its own challenges related to budget, advancement, and support.

It's no secret that writing centers are more often found in privileged spaces, more likely to exist at private universities than at two-year colleges (Salem, 2014). At some funding-strapped universities, a writing center can seem like an expendable luxury, even though those are places where students may need the resources most. It's my hope that workplace writing centers may signal the importance of this resource to universities. Perhaps if workplaces more clearly invest in their employees' writing skills with a writing center model, some universities may come a step closer to understanding the value of their own writing centers. Writing centers won't just appear as a service students may use in preparation for life after graduation—they may be a part of their professional lives someday, as well.

Expansion, innovation, and subversion are all at the heart of writing center work. And as Trimbur predicted in 2010, "writing centers have a lot to gain by expanding their work beyond campus" (pp. 89–90). Writing center professionals will always try to meet writers where they are. In recent years, we've already had to consider how we can reach across space (with virtual sessions), diverse populations and disciplines (multiliteracy centers), and time (asynchronous sessions). Our reach into the workplace could help an untapped pool of writers who, I have found, would be very eager for the company.

Comparable Models

Though writing centers, at least in name, have stopped short of workplace environments thus far, there are comparable models we can look to that *do* exist—or that existed some time ago. Most of the existing scholarly literature that I've come across related to consultant-based writing training in a workplace is about efforts conducted in the early 1990s (Karlson, 1991; Smart, 1999). One such effort was being carried out at the General Accounting Office, now known as the Government Accountability Office (GAO) in 1991[1]; another was led by Graham Smart at the Bank of Canada around the same time. My own workplace writing center experience has been in quasigovernmental and banking-related environments; the GAO and the Bank of Canada deal with similar types of writing and similar workplace hierarchies as those I am used to. Karlson notes the consequences and challenges that come with federal writing: "Because the GAO's writing leads, ostensibly, to actions by Congress, writers have to consider the special implications of public discourse (such as writing to both technical audiences and to the public)" (1991, p. 495). Writing simultaneously for internal and external audiences, or at least to an audience with a spectrum of subject familiarity, is a common workplace task. At the Bank of Canada, Smart focused his research on the ways in which employees collaboratively construct a narrative and negotiate meaning together. In much the same way as I did, Smart had to begin by immersing himself in the language of the workplace and to watch how "groups typically employ distinctive local discursive practices to create the specialized forms of knowledge needed to accomplish their work" (1999, p. 250). One particularly interesting note from Smart is that he did not need to introduce the concept of "telling the story" to the economists—it was a part of their local language already. This is a concept that I've heard touted in several industries: gather the data, then *tell the story* to the reader in a way that is clear and meaningful.

The GAO uses embedded, on-site consultants to help with staff writing. This team consisted of "two full-time employees devoted to writing training and a pool of 15 expert consultants who work[ed] part time" (1991, p. 494). The GAO's writing services began with a series of workshops deemed "highly successful"; however, these services were then passed off to the GAO's Training Institute (p. 494). And though Graham Smart published a few different pieces on his work with the Bank of Canada, he later returned to academia. It appears that neither Smart nor Karlson formed a relationship within the writing center community or joined any related professional organizations.

But the approaches that these pioneers considered and the philosophy they embraced can inform the model(s) that this book will suggest. Karlson's attempts to create partnerships between trainers and workplace writers mirror what we see in traditional writing centers. The GAO worked to make "the teaching seem less mysterious and the workplace more habitable" with "seminar participants engag[ing] in choices about language" in a more collaborative forum (1991, p. 495). This mutual respect for writers is vital to the work that is done at any writing center. The GAO's consultants also model "the importance of writing as a social activity"; Karlson explains that "through encounters with teams, with reviewers, and with individuals who have all sorts of quirks and strengths…they learn the value of diversity, the importance of context, and the limits of our knowledge about writing" (1991, p. 495). By encouraging new employees to talk to one another about the choices they make in their writing, we can similarly encourage them to think about the collaborative nature of meaning-making, and to think about how readers, reviewers, and their cowriters will interpret the text at hand.

It seems that the US GAO and the Bank of Canada have both maintained their writing-focused programs in some capacity (Dorothy Goldsmith, personal communication, July 22, 2019; Maren Hansen, personal communication,

July 31, 2019). The GAO has one or more communications analysts assigned to each mission team (i.e., a group made up of subject matter experts (SMEs) focusing on the same issue; there are about 2,100 analysts and approximately 70 communications analysts as of January 2020). They also have a robust writing curriculum and training program that offers about 15 different writing workshops to employees. Although the communications analysts will provide one-on-one guidance if specifically requested, this has not been a frequent method of training.

As of January 2020, the Bank of Canada *does* still provide one-on-one writing coaching, though they do not have any professional connections with writing center-related organizations. The lead writing consultant at the Bank of Canada, Maren Hansen, shared that her professional connections are mostly plain language groups (e.g., attending the Clarity 2018 conference), editors' groups, and the University of Ottawa's Centre for Continuing Education. In response to increased client demand, the team has since implemented six workshops covering topics such as clarity/readability, summarizing and synthesizing to add value, stages of the writing process, and the specific genres of presentations/slide decks, briefing notes, and email (Maren Hansen, personal communication, September 2021). These updates are significant because it seems that both organizations are still aligned with the stances put forth in the articles published by Karlson and Smart in the early 1990s. At the same time, neither organization has specifically connected with the writing center world or participated in its scholarship.

The IWCA website does include one other paper that describes a service somewhat similar to ours—Michael Erard's "Writing Centers in Professional Contexts" (2006). In 2006, Erard was employed at the Cain Research Center in the School of Nursing at the University of Texas at Austin. He was working with professionals on high-stakes documents rather than working with student writing; his description of an "accidental writing center" resonated with me at first. I recognized the hurdles that he faced in his environment, from encouraging professionals to trust his judgment to navigating confidentiality while still keeping his supervisors informed. However, based on Erard's description of the service, I had some trouble accepting it as a true writing center. He described his services:

> Faculty send me their documents via e-mail, I make corrections and queries with the 'track changes' function, then e-mail the document back... About one-third of the time, I contact authors during the editing process via email, phone, or face-too-face; otherwise, the work proceeds without any contact.

This, to me, sounds more like a developmental editing service. Though it seems that Erard was a valuable resource to his workplace, his main focus was not necessarily to improve writers' independent skills. Erard also posits that "professionals make reluctant students", which I think would be an unfair blanket statement for many workplaces. I will later touch on the identity shifts that writing consultants face when moving into tutoring in a professional environment; Erard indicates this challenge as well. However, I disagree with his notion that the "position would be impossible for a non-PhD to do". I think that a background in writing centers and/or rhetoric and composition are imperative, but excellent people skills are more important than a terminal degree. In the conclusion of Erard's paper, he describes the conditions that I agree work well for a workplace writing center: "I could see it working well in settings where employees write high-stakes persuasive texts for a variety of internal and external audiences". These are exactly the types of texts that many workplaces would be eager to have support for.

Writing Centers as a Valuable Workplace Resource

Having worked for both academic and nonacademic employers, I am interested in the gap in expectations between the two. Workplaces expect to hire people who are ready to perform on-the-job writing tasks skillfully without additional support. College and university professors are expected to prepare overloaded classes with the writing skills they need for any and all future industries...simultaneously. These expectations need to change if we truly want to see students succeed as they transition to the workplace (or to see new hires succeed as they navigate their new roles). First, let's consider the challenges that writers often confront as they enter the workforce or transition to a new industry.

Academic vs. Nonacademic Writing Styles

In general, much of what students are rewarded for in the classroom is later scolded in the workplace. Classroom settings tend to praise "sophisticated language" and an abundance of detail, both of which can be detrimental to the quick, easy reader comprehension valued in the workplace (McNamara, Crossley, & McCarthy, 2010, p. 57). There is also evidence to suggest that the errors that irk professors are very different from those eschewed in nonacademic workplaces (Boettger & Emory Moore, 2018). I don't point this out to put more blame on academics; rather, I think we frequently overlook the importance of different conventions in each space, and how highly specialized forms of writing can be for particular workspaces. At many universities and colleges, business communication courses and freshman composition are increasingly "taught by graduate teaching assistants, who may have little professional experience outside academia and thus little experience with the kinds of business-oriented writing that they are asked to teach and that students need to practice and develop" (Mackiewicz, 2012, p. 233). Professors with a variety of backgrounds and past experience may also find themselves choosing between inadequate instructional resources. Particularly within engineering departments, many communications textbooks include examples of memos and other forms of writing that follow humanities conventions too closely, and that reflect professors' ideals rather than practicing engineers' ideals (Amare & Brammar, 2005; Wolfe, 2009). The resources and instruction methods available to professors can also mislead students to think that they can rely on plugging information into templates when they arrive in the workplace (Cox, Ortmeier-Hooper, & Tirabassi, 2009; Wiggins, 2009). The questions that I heard most frequently in my own writing classrooms as a student were typically related to concerns that were even more superficial than following a template. In an attempt to earn the highest grade possible, students learn to cling to measurable direction related to minimum page count, spacing, and margin size; none of this is very helpful in a nonacademic workplace (Cox et al., 2009; Steiner, 2011).

Inauthentic Writing Tasks

Though many professors attempt to replicate real-world prompts and assignments as closely as they can, it is still impossible to truly represent the culture shock that students commonly face when moving from the classroom to a high-stakes workplace. When students transition into the workplace, they are drawing on years of experience that typically involved "writing to please a single-person audience (the professor) and to earn a grade" (Quick, 2012, p. 233). Writing becomes a way to convey as much information to the professor as possible, as opposed to guiding a reader toward comprehension or persuasion. Every time I teach a writing workshop, I remind my colleagues that once they have left school, they will *never* have to write something merely for the sake of...writing something. They will always be writing to inform, or to persuade, or to apologize, or to ask, or to appeal. Workplace writing is contextual, task-driven, and it involves real and complex audiences (Kryder, 1995). Even more pointedly: "Real writers are trying to make a difference, find their true audience, and cause some result in their readership...what few young writers learn is that there are consequences for succeeding or failing as a real writer" (Wiggins, 2009, p. 30). Rather than writing to a singular expert (e.g., a professor), writers in the workplace often know more about the topic than their audience and must think carefully about how to choose and clearly relay information (Cox et al., 2009, p. 73). At times, these audiences are multitiered, with different levels of comprehension among them. It is not enough to be able to use language as a vehicle for technical information. Writers need to relay complex, high-stakes concepts in a way that is, at the end of the day, not only understandable, but "appealing to other human beings" (McCloskey, 1998, p. 107).

Collaboration and Diversity

Workplace writing is often more collaborative than students may expect (Mabrito, 1999). Many professors anticipate the amount of collaborative work their students will face, and they try to prepare them with collaborative assignments. But the consequences and challenges of collaborative writing can be very different between the classroom and the workplace. As was my experience, students tend to divide up collaborative work and complete portions on their own, with little actual collaboration between them (Bremner, 2012). Though students may have the opportunity to evaluate one another's contributions in a way that reflects their final grades, this still doesn't reflect the demand for true collaboration in many workplace assignments, nor the consequences of poor individual performance (e.g., perpetual slackers don't benefit from grading curves—they get fired). Though many of the reports I've worked with are written by a number of different people, each working on specific areas, they must communicate frequently with one another to determine how these different areas impact the message for the audience. A great deal of work goes into making sure the final document is clear, reads with the singular voice of an authority, and paces out important information for audience comprehension.

Though many students have their first exposure to diverse populations when they arrive at college campuses, postgrads may later struggle with the transition from campus cultures to workplace cultures and the even greater diversity that comes with it (Barnett, 2012). In the workplace, employees often represent a vast range of ages, socioeconomic status, language backgrounds, "disciplinary background, work styles, experience and motives" (Bremner, 2012, p. 123). Though I had a diverse set of friends in my hometown and in my higher education experience, I still found myself navigating my diverse workplace somewhat uncertainly when I first arrived. I was used to leading writing consultations with people from a variety of different backgrounds, but I was still thrown by the dynamic of trying to earn the respect of people who had decades' worth of experience beyond my own.

Bringing Real-World Context into the Classroom

Even when professors refer to conventions specific to different disciplines, the workforce can still remain abstractly defined without the actual context at hand (Bourelle, 2015, p. 407) and without subject matter expertise and experience to inform language use (Conrad, 2018, p. 68). Some business communication classes have found ways to provide at least some real-world exposure and context to their students. Though translating knowledge to the workplace is still a challenge, some courses are closer than others at presenting workplace-relevant instruction (Clokie & Fourie, 2016; Moshiri & Cardon, 2014). In general, it seems that the more professors are able to connect students with information specific to their particular career interests, the easier the transition will be when they enter the workforce. For some students, this may involve linking assignments to clinical practice or other experience (Clarke, Schull, Coleman, Pitt, & Manathunga, 2013). Internships are an especially valuable opportunity for students to connect their writing instruction with workplace contexts and genre-specific writing tasks (Bourelle, 2014; Conrad, 2018).

Colleges and universities, of course, can have vastly different access to internship opportunities for students. And even when access is available, there are some aspects of workplace writing that are impossible to replicate outside of the workplace itself. Even when mentors provide frameworks for workplace writing, each workplace has its own specific context (Lucas & Rawlins, 2015). And "even with an abundance of case study documents and scenarios meant to reproduce the real world", professors still cannot "recreate the complexity and dynamics of the workplace, particularly of changes in planning due to new-client or workplace-based contingencies" (Kohn, 2015, p. 169). Workplace writing genres are generally taught as static (Kohn, 2015) and as one-way exchanges (Moshiri & Cardon, 2014, p. 322). But workplace writing is much more interactive, especially with the immediacy of instant messaging, email, and social media. Even more traditional documents like monthly reports require "constant customization, constant boundary-crossing, and constant ethos-building" (Spinuzzi, 2010, p. 378).

Workplace as a Learning Site

It's not fair or possible to expect business communication professors to be able to completely equip students for the many paths they will take throughout their careers. Instead, workplaces should recognize the abundant learning opportunities in new employees' first weeks on the job (Cyphert, Holke-Farnam, Dodge, Lee, & Rosol, 2019). The "rhetorical adaptability" that we encourage students to have in the workplace grows out of ongoing exposure to workplace culture (Quick, 2012, p. 234). Many workplaces also have their own unique forms of writing or yearly writing tasks that would be impossible to anticipate outside of this environment. For example, while students may have experience receiving professors' feedback on memos and reports, they may find themselves learning to create different documents related to year-end performance or 360-degree reviews (Yu, 2010). I've seen my own workplace writing center consultants invited by HR departments on several occasions to help teach employees how to improve these specific (and frequently changing!) tasks. It's not uncommon for workplaces to recognize that they need to have *some* form of writing support available to employees. But such support typically involves proofreading, copy-editing, and rewriting, rather than teaching employees the kinds of rhetorical adaptability they need. That's what makes a workplace writing center a very different resource from those that most workplaces have seen before.

Traditional Workplace Writing Resources

When I have collaborated with workplaces to create writing centers, I have noticed that the resources previously available were somewhat transactional in nature. Typically, writers would turn in a product to someone in the department (e.g., a team lead, a manager, or a perceived stronger writer), and see a clean copy later on in the review process. Researchers would write a paper, email it to editors within an Internal Communications or Pubic Affairs department, and then click "accept all changes" once they received the marked-up copy. And in years when writing was deemed a higher priority, sometimes a writing professional from a local university would be contracted to lead a one-off writing workshop. Although technical writers' and editors' roles have shifted somewhat with the introduction of new technologies, they still find themselves rewriting pieces that originate in other departments (Hayhoe, 2007).

Moving Away from Transactional Approaches

There is plenty of research that attempts to capture the frustration that comes with some of these transactional modes. SMEs frequently underestimate or misunderstand the work that technical writers do; such oversights have left technical writers "struggling to achieve mature professional status" (Hallier & Malone, 2012, p. 29) and repeatedly defending the legitimacy and value of their work (Henning & Bemer, 2016, p. 312). When SMEs are able to pass along their writing to an editor or technical writer, the relationship between the two parties can be tense. Editors often find themselves with limited authority when they don't have the opportunity to communicate directly with SMEs; SMEs may dismiss suggested changes as inapplicable, whether they truly are or not (Lanier, 2009). It isn't uncommon to hear technical communicators complain about SMEs being unappreciative, "difficult and contentious" (Rice-Bailey, 2016, p. 231), rude, or noncommunicative (Lee and Mehlenbacher, 2000). Without communication between groups and an understanding of what the other does, it can be easy for SMEs to see technical writers and communicators as a black box that merely slows down their processes.

Such traditional, transactional approaches can also create challenges for SMEs. When SMEs are unable to participate in the revision or rewriting of their own work, they can find themselves losing control of their products. In some contexts, direct proofreading can introduce "errors into the writer's text, making a poor text even worse in places" (Harwood, 2018, p. 474). I frequently remind the writers I work with that they truly *do not want* me to rewrite their pieces for them—I assure them that they have a much better grasp on the information, and my role is merely to make sure I (and the reader) understand what they are attempting to communicate. Losing control of their work can also be demotivating; one study found that "not seeing the fruits of their labor, having to focus solely on efficiency and savings, and lacking recognition decreased employees' motivation" (Batova, 2018, p. 335). I have found this to be the case in various workplaces, as well. Though I commonly hear report reviewers express frustration with rewriting reports, I quickly found that the original writers tend to be frustrated with the process, too. When I've surveyed staff in different workplaces, many reported that they were discouraged when they saw their final reports and barely recognized any of the language. They understood that they clearly weren't turning in what was expected, but they had no idea what changes were being made or why they were being made.

Even those who took the time to review the tracked changes in their documents found themselves overwhelmed by the volume of revisions. There had been no attempt to invite them into a conversation about clear expectations, or to deliberately move past the long-accepted, transactional approach.

Moving Toward Transformational Approaches

Some studies within the field of education have looked at the impact of transactional versus transformational learning. In a transactional approach, teachers feed passive students knowledge; in a transformational approach, students are empowered to improve their own skills, work independently, and self-assess their progress and needs (Balloo, Evans, Hughes, Zhu, & Winstone, 2018). The same framework of transactional-versus-transformational also appears in studies of leadership styles. In one such study, transactional methods were defined as being "based around monitoring and control" (Waddell & Pio, 2015, p. 470), while transformational methods were described as "the embedding of knowledge within the organisation, the reactivation of knowledge for future use and the willingness to challenge and test ideas and assumptions" (p. 471).

I can see editing, technical writing, and other traditional approaches to "fixing" department writing as falling into the category of *transactional* approaches. The knowledge—or sometimes, just the "fix"—is handed to the writer, without much attempt at explaining the change or improving the writer's understanding. This sounds precisely like the product-focused mindset that North warned against in 1984. I see workplace writing centers as landing more squarely within a *transformational* approach. The goal is to change the writers: to make them understand the gap between expectation and performance, as well as, over time, how to bridge the gap themselves. We work *with* and *alongside* writers, not *for* them.

Carolyn Miller seems to encourage a more transformational approach in "A Humanistic Rationale for Technical Writing" (1979). Within a technical writing classroom, she argues that we should extend beyond teaching "a set of techniques for accommodating slippery words to intractable things" toward "how to belong to a community" (p. 617). Miller knows we must still teach traditional writing rules and genres, but she pushes the focus deeper into "the concepts, values, traditions, and style which permit identification with that community and determine the success or failure of communication" (p. 617). In other words: We should be inviting our writers into this conversation, negotiating what it means to be a part of a community, rather than simply sharing corrections and rules.

A writing center model can bring this approach back out of the technical writing classroom and into individual workplaces. In some workplaces, it may help to tie this to a larger process change. With changes in review processes and document sharing technologies, some editors have managed to step into more of a coaching role, guiding SMEs through new procedures (Lanier, 2009).

Ultimately, the goal is to begin shifting responsibility back to the writer so that they maintain control of the product and develop a sense of pride in its quality.

To be clear, I'm not arguing that all editors or technical writers should step into coaching roles instead. There is incredible value in making sure a clean, polished written deliverable reaches stakeholders, and the expertise that editors and technical writers hold lacks the recognition it deserves. But when editors or technical writers have to take on deeper and deeper revisions, and even full rewrites, processes can become inefficient, more laborious than necessary, and discouraging for them *and* the writer. But if a second resource is available—one that seeks to build writers' skills and transform their understanding of the work they produce—editors can focus on producing clean, solid products, and writers can focus on crafting and controlling their messages.

Offering Guidance, Inspiring Revision

When revision processes can be passed along to an editor or another party, it becomes easier for writers to dismiss their importance or to ignore opportunities for learning and improvement. Even when writers are charged with implementing guidance provided by reviewers, they tend to focus on surface-level comments related to format or surface-level errors (Mackiewicz, 2014). It may be because these types of superficial changes are easier to apply to a text; it may also be because writers are able to recognize these comments as a product of reviewers' commodity work (p. 441). In classrooms, it's been indicated that "students underst[and] the reasons for comments only half the time", and the comments they see as "rule based" can be dismissed as "not worthy of in-depth understanding" (Taylor, 2011, p. 161). The best understood comments, on the other hand, included those with "readerly and coaching comments about development of ideas" or that provided "explanations of the comment's reason" (p. 161).

Traditionally, editors and technical writers produce clean copies of documents or copies marked-up with written comments, but this may also hinder writers' ability to understand and learn from revisions. Writers are more likely to learn from feedback when it is available multimodally, accounting for differing learning styles and preferences (Crews & Wilkinson, 2010, p. 410). In a writing center consultation, this becomes possible. Rather than marking up a writer's paper, we talk through possible revisions. We also allow time for writers to make changes themselves, if they find hands-on implementation most helpful. Feedback can be demonstrated visually on paper or whiteboards, described orally, or coached indirectly. And when writers are present in these moments, we can use their preferences to inform our feedback styles.

Some workplaces attempt to provide varied instruction or immediate feedback by hiring a writing expert to lead a one-time writing workshop, or by buying a software package that provides writing feedback. The trouble is that these outside consultants are expensive, are not necessarily familiar with the localized context and industry specifics, and are unhelpful for anyone who is not present at the workshop. Any employee who is traveling for work, taking sick or vacation time, or who is hired after the workshop will not benefit from a one-time offering. And even if we manage to encourage a significant population of employees to attend, skill decay is a major concern (Salas, Tannenbaum, Kraiger, & Smith-Jentsch, 2012, p. 83). New software programs such as Grammarly provide more ongoing support, but they tend to be limited in their effectiveness. Though Grammarly can quickly provide a writer with a great volume of feedback, it isn't intuitive enough to streamline similar comments. It can't "expand its range of knowledge, lower its comment count, or otherwise change its approach", all of which can be overwhelming and demotivating to writers (Dembsey, 2017, p. 76).

Exigency

Now is an important time to consider a workplace writing center. Rapid changes in technology and available communication platforms affect the ways we express our ideas, presenting challenges for writers. Increased globalization of the workplace means not only communicating across language barriers at times but also making multilingual employees feel welcomed and supported. And as more and more workspaces begin considering ways to create a fair and safe environment for employees regardless of their background, a writing center can help everyone to communicate in a way that is clearer, more powerful, and more inclusive. It's time for companies to "acknowledge their role in developing employees' writing" (Lentz, 2013, p. 485). In 1995, Kryder predicted that learning would "become the competitive advantage" for workplaces (p. 53), and we are now seeing this in practice as traditional production economies shift to knowledge economies (Lentz, 2013, p. 487).

Changes in Technology

While changes in technology can help us communicate with more people more quickly, these sudden shifts can also present new challenges for employees. When a new program, process, or media is introduced in an organization, it can "lead users simply to apply ineffective habits of use from old technologies to new ones" (Yates, Orlikowski, & Okamura, 1999, p. 100). Organizations can also struggle when employees adopt technology at different rates: I have heard more seasoned coworkers lament the years when some staff refused to learn word processing software instead of handwriting reports or dictating them to a secretary. Organizations are more likely to successfully navigate such transitions when supervisors stress related benefits, such as increased efficiency and speed (Lanier, 2009, p. 475). Some technology-driven changes, such as the transition from handwriting to typing, can also result in writing of "significantly greater conceptual complexity" (Van Der Steen, Samuelson, & Thomson, 2017, p. 297).

But in many cases, these available benefits can be hindered by insufficient writing support and guidance. Email has become one of the most-cited areas of concern for organizations (Gray, Emerson, & MacKay, 2005, p. 434). An organization's particular "email writing practices, including when, who, and why to CC, as appropriate" remain highly contextual and ill-defined (Machili, Angouri, & Harwood, 2019, p. 26). Not only are most workplaces failing to provide training for employees on local email communication, they also tend to not have any standards in place (Gygi & Zachry, 2010, p. 361). The same appears to be true for newer communication mediums such as PowerPoint, where employees are learning largely by trial and error (Hertz, van Woerkum, & Kerkhof, 2015). Presenters' experience tends to inform their practices, with "beginners us[ing] twice as many words per minute as advanced presenters" (p. 292). I've observed this among my own colleagues—newer employees tend to pack slides with text, even if the presentation is intended for an upper-level executive. Being able to provide them with clear guidance and immediate feedback has helped streamline presentations in our department considerably.

While workplaces know intuitively that IT departments are necessary to help employees learn how to leverage new technology effectively and securely, they fail to provide adequate training on how and when to use various tools. Though the workforce has become increasingly mobile, important messages are often best handled in phone calls or face-to-face conversations (Kiddie, 2014, p. 83). The value of having a conversation versus creating a paper trail was an important lesson that I was lucky to have shared with me early in my career, but not all managers provide such guidance. There are also increasingly subtle ways in which technology can influence the relationship between writer and reader. Though, for example, there seems to be no difference in perception when a writer clearly sends an email from an iPhone, the impression can still be filtered through markers as slight as the writer's punctuation use and perceived gender (Marlow, Lacerenza, & Iwig, 2018, p. 160).

Globalization

With technology connecting us more quickly and easily, the workforce has become increasingly globalized. Writers collaborate across time zones, language barriers, and cultural norms. These complicating factors—especially those related to differences in time zones and schedules—can make it easier for colleagues to communicate asynchronously in writing, at times. This places even greater importance on international communication's "clarity of purpose, simplicity of prose, correctness of spelling and grammar, and diplomacy in word choice" (Kryder, 1995, p. 50). Though some workplaces employ translators and technical communicators, others pass vital communication tasks to professionals with no formal background in communication. In China, SMEs tend to be the ones to develop technical manuals (Ding, 2010, p. 306); when I worked with one organization in Southeast Asia, I found that many high-profile speeches were written by employees with no rhetorical or speech-writing training. In the latter case, midlevel employees would receive emails late at night to develop a speech by morning; this was, of course, a distressing, difficult, and time-consuming task that was creating rifts in the organization. These informal speechwriters had nowhere to turn for support or advocacy. And in many international workplaces, it is true that even as one advances throughout their career, "the relative importance of technical skills declines, while the importance of communication skills increases" (Gayathridevi & Deepa, 2015, p. 95).

Even beyond language barriers, differences in culture can have deep rhetorical implications. In different nations, ethos can vary widely between voices. As one example, Italian and American reports tend to favor managers' voices and voices of authorities, while Chinese reports tend to rely on client or external voices; in each culture, these voices hold different rhetorical weight (Bondi & Yu, 2019, p. 193). Developing an understanding of different cultures' unique communication patterns can improve relationships in cross-cultural interactions, and can also work to reduce prejudice (Jarvis Kwadzo Bokor, 2011). There is also other evidence that as we continue to communicate cross-culturally, rhetorical patterns are converging (Wang, 2010, p. 92). Shifts on either (or both!) ends of communication can leave writers with the added task of trying to adapt to these changes. We can't expect employees to arrive in the workplace knowing how to navigate all of this in our site-specific contexts. Additional challenges exist for employees who have received their education outside of their country of employment; one study reports that Lebanese instructors at a school of business recognized their students' struggles with English writing, but they did not feel it was their responsibility to teach writing (Annous & Nicolas, 2015, p. 103). Rhetorical adaptability requires some amount of training and direction, and even when employees haven't been adequately prepared in their formal education, this "can primarily be learned on the job" (Kankaanranta & Louhiala-Salminen, 2010, p. 208). We don't have to worry so much about making sure all employees arrive with the ability to perform at the level we desire; we need to offer the types of resources that can help employees improve. Even those who report struggling to write in a nonnative language seem "to report that their success as scholarly authors depends on knowing how to find the resources they need to compensate for this perceived deficit" (Koerber & Graham, 2017, p. 84). A writing center that offers both group workshops and individualized, ongoing instruction could be one of these promising resources.

Democratization of the Workplace

Providing writing support in our workplaces is about more than just saving money or encouraging efficient production. It's about creating the kinds of environments that we want to work and live in, and how we include others in those spaces. When I was working at Salisbury University's Writing Center, we had a small cohort of international students from South Korea who would visit at least weekly. These students didn't know where else to turn for additional practice with English writing and conversation. Most of the time, they just wanted to practice speaking with us. They knew, as many diverse students and workers know, how much their communication can impact the way their competence is perceived (Ortiz, Region-Sebest, & MacDermott, 2016, p. 327). One morning, they brought the tutors on duty homemade kimchi (a tough sell at 8 AM, but delicious nonetheless), just to show their gratitude for the service. I was instantly reminded of The Olgas, the stories we shared, the ways we learned from each other, and the ways we all were better off for it.

Once students leave academic environments, they often find themselves with limited (or no!) opportunities for support. This lack can create a massive and unfair disadvantage as they enter the workplace and navigate their professional careers. Research across several decades shows that employees' writing and communication skills factor into their rate of promotion, so weaker writing skills can impact the course of one's career (Aldrich, 1982; Lamar Reinsch & Gardner, 2014). Employees who demonstrate outstanding writing skills may find themselves facing a different disadvantage entirely. Jennifer Mallette's 2017 case study highlighted how one woman, a "highly skilled, talented engineer" felt held back in her career because "her writing ability caused her to be assigned more writing and given less design-related tasks" (pp. 438–439). To make up for her teammates' weaker writing skills, the female engineer carried the team's invisible labor and became dissatisfied with her job and the recognition she received—so much so that she ended up leaving the field entirely. Without a resource in place to provide writing support for the weaker teammates and to hold them accountable, a series of shifted responsibilities led to losing one of the strongest employees (and, arguably, a lack of improvement among those who avoided writing).

Mallette argued that the engineer's gender made her a target for the invisible work of writing; there is an abundance of other examples of the ways that marginalized or underrepresented groups can suffer if we do not invest in services that help manage inequitable skillsets and prejudices in the workplace. Writing and communication styles reflect cultural values and norms, impacting the ways in which employees assimilate into an organization (Sollitto & Cranmer, 2019, p. 287). And all too frequently, "workers with limited literacy skills can be held responsible for poor economic performance at an enterprise, industry, and national level" (Clayson, 2018, p. 561). These workers can be blamed based on their ethnicity, with the assumption that their English is inadequate; their disposition, with the assumption that their work ethic is poor; or their socioeconomic circumstances, with the assumption that they do not or have not valued education (p. 561). Employees' age can also be a source of discrimination and misplaced judgment. As millennials (and now, Gen Z) enter the workforce, it can be easy for managers to assume that the newest generation's writing is poor, when in truth, this group is adapting to entirely new rhetorical situations (Omilion-Hodges & Sugg, 2019, p. 92). Likewise, older generations may find themselves answering to younger managers who underestimate their familiarity with technology or more cutting-edge skills.

Though some stereotypical traits may have some link to different generations, "the extent to which [they] will surface can depend a great deal on what the company does, how big it is, how successful it is, and how it is managed" (Rentz, 2015, p. 162). If we leverage judgments against generations instead of providing them with any individual help that they need, we can greatly limit the potential of our workforce.

I may have grown up wanting to be "a writer who helps people", but it's the "who helps people" part that has come to matter most to me. The guidance that technical writing, rhetoric, communications, and composition specialists can provide in the workplace can go so far beyond rewriting or correcting writers' work for them. Instead, "as a humanistic discipline, our focus should be squarely on improving the human experience for the oppressed" (Jones, 2016, p. 357). We have the opportunity to empower people by teaching them what we know and shifting their viewpoints. All too often, new employees arrive to the workforce and see only barriers, wondering how they can or if they are even allowed to share the same language as experts (Falconer, 2019). If we can establish resources embedded within workplace communities, we can remind each generation that this language does not come naturally to anyone, really, but that we can support them through joining the community and earning a part in it (Falconer, 2019).

The Next Unknowns

As I write this in the spring of 2021, the world is still reeling from the Covid-19 pandemic. No workplace escaped its effects, and many are reevaluating what employees' relationship to the workplace will be. Some industries are questioning the viability of the five-day workweek, and many are considering a restructuring of work arrangements. One study of knowledge workers found that just "12% want to return to full-time office work, and 72% want a hybrid remote-office model moving forward" (Fogarty et al., 2020). Workplaces are redesigning physical spaces, moving away from crowded, open-concept office plans; ideally, there will be an increased focus on facilitating meaningful and safe interactions (Booker & Kargbo, 2021). Some are allowing employees to continue working remotely full-time, or to shift to a hybrid model of onsite and offsite work. And still others are creating offset shifts to minimize the number of people in the office at once.

One thing we can be sure of is the fact that workplaces will look vastly different from one another and from anything that we could have imagined a decade ago. And because none of us could have predicted these sudden changes, we should also accept that the next iterations of workplace culture and logistics could also take us by surprise. Offices are being redesigned not just for public health reasons, but for pending climate changes, too (Vaughn, 2020). Many workplaces have found that they can simply cut costs by downsizing their physical office spaces and allowing for more flexible work arrangements (Fogarty et al., 2020). Of course, not all workers will have the luxury and trust of working outside of a physical workplace. But employees deemed essential for onsite work will still need to develop remote communication skills to continue working with those now offsite.

In any of these situations, a workplace writing center remains a valuable investment. Writing centers have been navigating remote services and support for years, and they can help writers to overcome the communication challenges that come from a dispersed workforce. While employers adapt to what is being billed as the *new normal*, there is an opportunity to pitch workplace writing centers as a resource that can support and ease these transitions.

Summary

Throughout their century-long and varied history, writing centers have emerged and adapted to meet people where they are. The goal has always been to help writers improve and thrive in the challenges of their current environment.

While many professors and teachers do their best to introduce students to the types of "real-world" writing they'll face after school, it's unrealistic and unfair to place this burden on them alone. Workplaces should take an active role in helping employees to join their unique discourse communities. Writing centers can serve as a sustainable resource to help new hires transition to the workplace, and to help employees of varied experience and backgrounds communicate more effectively.

Traditional writing support in the workplace—when it even exists—is typically transactional in nature. A writer may generate an initial written product, but then an editor or technical writer takes over and eventually hands back a new written product. Or an outside writing expert may be commissioned by a workplace to give a one-off workshop, during which writers are expected to take this knowledge and apply it consistently. Writing centers, on the other hand, take a transformational approach. The goal moves beyond "fixing" documents and toward building writers' skills so that the documents they write improve over time.

There has never been a better time for workplaces to consider investing in a workplace writing center. Particularly in knowledge industries, workplaces are evolving more and more rapidly. Changes in technology impact not just the ways we complete our work, but the ways that we communicate [about] our work. The globalization of the workforce has challenged writers to communicate with more and more diverse groups of people. Providing writers with support to write clearly and efficiently is one way that we can help democratize our workplaces.

Though it's hard to know what the next evolutions of the workplace will be, many academic writing centers already stand as excellent examples of adaptability. No matter the work at hand or the physical office environment, any workplace could benefit from having their own writing center.

Note

1 Per the agency's website: "GAO provides Congress, the heads of executive agencies, and the public with timely, fact-based, non-partisan information that can be used to improve government and save taxpayers billions of dollars" (U.S. Government Accountability Office, 2019).

References

Aldrich, P. G. (1982). Adult writers: Some reasons for ineffective writing on the job. *College Composition and Communication, 33*(3), 284–287.

Amare, N., & Brammar, C. (2005). Perceptions of memo quality: A case of engineering practitioners, professors, and students. *Journal of Writing and Technical Communication, 35*(2), 179–190.

Annous, S., & Nicolas, M. O. (2015). Academic territorial borders: A look at the writing ethos in business courses in an environment in which English is a foreign language. *Journal of Business and Technical Communication, 29*(1), 93–111. https://doi.org/10.1177/1050651914548457

Balloo, K., Evans, C., Hughes, A., Zhu, X., & Winstone, N. (2018). Transparency isn't spoon-feeding: How a transformative approach to the use of explicit assessment criteria can support student self-regulation. *Frontiers in Education, 3*(69).

Barnett, K. (2012). Student interns' socially constructed work realities: Narrowing the work expectation-reality gap. *Business Communication Quarterly, 75*(3), 271–290. https://doi.org/10.1177/1080569912441360

Batova, T. (2018). Work motivation in the rhetoric of component content management. *Journal of Business and Technical Communication, 32*(3), 308–346. https://doi.org/10.1177/1050651918762030

Berlin, J. A. (1987). *Rhetoric and reality: Writing instruction in American colleges, 1900–1985.* Carbondale: Southern Illinois University Press.

Boettger, R. K., & Emory Moore, L. (2018). Analyzing error perception and recognition among professional communication practitioners and academics. *Business and Professional Communication Quarterly, 81*(4), 462–484. https://doi.org/10.1177/2329490618803740

Bondi, M., & Yu, D. (2019). Textual voices in corporate reporting: A cross-cultural analysis of Chinese, Italian, and American CSR reports. *International Journal of Business Communication, 56*(2), 173–197. https://doi-org.lib-e2.lib.ttu.edu/10.1177/2329488418784690

Booker, C. & Kargbo, C. (2021, March 14). Will workers return to re-imagined offices post-pandemic? PBS. Retrieved from https://www.pbs.org/newshour/show/will-workers-return-to-re-imagined-offices-post-pandemic

Bourelle, T. (2014). New perspectives on the technical communication internship: Professionalism in the workplace. *Journal of Technical Writing & Communication, 44*(2), 171–189. https://doi-org.libe2.lib.ttu.edu/10.2190/TW.44.2.d

Bourelle, T. (2015). Writing in the professions: An internship for interdisciplinary students. *Business and Professional Communication Quarterly, 78*(4), 407–427. https://doi.org/10.1177/2329490615589172

Bremner, S. (2012). Socialization and the acquisition of professional discourse: A case study in the PR industry. *Written Communication, 29*(1), 7–32. https://doi.org/10.1177/0741088311424866

Carino, P. (Spring 1995). Early writing centers: Toward a history. *The Writing Center Journal, 15*(2), 103–115. Retrieved from www.jstor.org/stable/43441973

Carino, P. (Fall 1996). Open admissions and the construction of writing center history: A tale of three models. *The Writing Center Journal, 17*(1), 30–48. Retrieved from www.jstor.org/stable/43442014.

Carpenter, R., Whiddon, S., & Morin, C. (2017). "For writing centers, by writing centers": A new model for certification via regional organizations. *WLN: A Journal of Writing Center Scholarship, 42*(1–2), 2–9. Retrieved from https://wlnjournal.org/archives/v42/42.1-2.pdf.

Clarke, P., Schull, D., Coleman, G., Pitt, R., & Manathunga, C. (2013). Enhancing professional skills of veterinary technical students: linking assessment and clinical practice in a communications course. *Assessment & Evaluation in Higher Education, 38*(3), 273–287.

Clayson, A. (2018). Distributed cognition and embodiment in text planning: A situated study of collaborative writing in the workplace. *Written Communication, 35*(2), 155–181. https://doi.org/10.1177/0741088317753348

Clokie, T. L., & Fourie, E. (2016). Graduate employability and communications competence: Are undergraduates taught relevant skills? *Business and Professional Communication Quarterly, 79*(4), 442–463. https://doi.org/10.1177/2329490616657635

Conrad, S. (2018). The use of passives and impersonal style in civil engineering writing. *Journal of Business and Technical Communication, 32*(1), 38–76. https://doi.org/10.1177/1050651917729864

Cox, M., Ortmeier-Hooper, C., & Tirabassi, K. E. (2009). Teaching writing for the "real world": Community and workplace writing. *The English Journal, 98*(5), 72–80.

Crews, T. B., & Wilkinson, K. (2010). Students' perceived preference for visual and auditory assessment with e-handwritten feedback. *Business and Professional Communication Quarterly, 73*(4), 399–412. https://journals-sagepub-com.libe2.lib.ttu.edu/doi/pdf/10.1177/1080569910385566

Cyphert, D., Holke-Farnam, C., Dodge, E. N., Lee, W. E., & Rosol, S. (2019). Communication activities in the 21st century business environment. *Business and Professional Communication Quarterly, 82*(2), 169–201. https://doi.org/10.1177/2329490619831279

Dembsey, J. M. (2017). Closing the Grammarly® gaps: A study of claims and feedback from an online grammar program. *Writing Center Journal, 36*(1), 63–100.

Ding, H. (2010). Technical communication instruction in China: Localized programs and alternative models. *Technical Communication Quarterly, 19*(3), 300–317. https://doi-org.libe2.lib.ttu.edu/10.1080/10572252.2010.481528

Ede, L. (1989). Writing as a social process: A theoretical foundation for writing centers? *The Writing Center Journal, 9*(2), 3–13. Retrieved from http://www.jstor.org/stable/43444122

Erard, M. (2006). Writing centers in professional contexts. Retrieved from http://writingcenters.org/writing-centers-in-professional-contexts-by-michael-erard/.

Falconer, H. M. (2019). "I think when I speak, I don't sound like that": The influence of social positioning on rhetorical skill development in science. *Written Communication, 36*(1), 9–37. https://doi.org/10.1177/0741088318804819

Fogarty, P., Frantz, S., Hirschfeld, J., Keating, S., Lafont, E., Lufkin, B., Mishael, R., Ponnavolu, V., Savage, M., & Turits, M. (2020, October 23). Coronavirus: How the world of work may change forever. *BBC*. Retrieved from https://www.bbc.com/worklife/article/20201023-coronavirus-how-will-the-pandemic-change-the-way-we-work.

Gayathridevi, K. S., & Deepa, R. (2015). Effectiveness of a business communication course: Evidence from a business school in India. *Business and Professional Communication Quarterly, 78*(1), 94–103. https://doi.org/10.1177/2329490614563567

Geller, A. E., & Denny, H. (2013). Of ladybugs, low status, and loving the job: Writing center professionals navigating their careers. *Writing Center Journal, 33*(1), 96–129.

Geller, A. E., Eodice, M., Condon, F., Carroll, M., & Boquet, E. H. (2007). *The everyday writing center: A community of practice.* Logan: Utah State University Press.

Gray, F. E., Emerson, L., & MacKay, B. (2005, December). Meeting the demands of the workplace: Science students and written skills. *Journal of Science Education and Technology, 14*(4). Retrieved from https://www.jstor.org/stable/40186675.

Gygi, K., & Zachry, M. (2010). Productive tensions and the regulatory work of genres in the development of an engineering communication workshop in a transnational corporation. *Journal of Business and Technical Communication, 24*(3), 358–381. https://doi.org/10.1177/1050651910363365

Hallier, P., & Malone, E. (2012). Light's "Technical Writing and Professional Status": Fifty years later. *Technical Communication, 59*(1), 29–31. Retrieved from http://www.jstor.org/stable/43092918

Harris, M. (Spring 1997). Open admissions and the construction of a writing center history: A tale of three models. *The Writing Center Journal, 17*(2), 134–140. Retrieved from www.jstor.org/stable/43442026.

Harwood, N. (2018). What do proofreaders of student writing to do a master's essay? Differing interventions, worrying findings. *Written Communication, 35*(4), 474–530. https://doi.org/10.1177/0741088318786236

Hayhoe, G. F. (2007). The future of technical writing and editing. *Technical Communication, 54*(3), 281–282.

Henning, T., & Bemer, A. (2016). Reconsidering power and legitimacy in technical communication: A case for enlarging the definition of technical communication. *Journal of Technical Writing and Communication, 46*(3), 311–341. https://doi.org/10.1177/0047281616639484

Hertz, B., van Woerkum, C., & Kerkhof, P. (2015). Why do scholars use PowerPoint the way they do? *Business and Professional Communication Quarterly, 78*(3), 273–291. https://doi.org/10.1177/2329490615589171

Jarvis Kwadzo Bokor, M. (2011). Connecting with the "other" in technical communication: world Englishes and ethos transformation of U.S. native English-speaking students. *Technical Communication Quarterly, 20*(2), 208–237. https://doi-org.libe2.lib.ttu.edu/10.1080/10572252.2011.551503

Jones, N. N. (2016). The Technical communicator as advocate: Integrating a social justice approach in technical communication. *Journal of Technical Writing and Communication, 46*(3), 342–361. https://doi.org/10.1177/0047281616639472

Kankaanranta, L., & Louhiala-Salminen (2010). English? Oh-it's just work!: A study of BELF users' perceptions. *English for Specific Purposes, 29*, 204–209.

Karlson, K. J. (1991, November). Writing training: Collaboration between academy and government agency. *Technical Communication, 38*(4), 493–497. Retrieved from https://www.jstor.org/stable/43095824.

Kent, R. (2006). *A guide to creating student-staffed writing centers.* New York: Peter Lang, Inc.

Kiddie, T. J. (2014). Text(ing) in context: The future of workplace communication in the United States. *Business and Professional Communication Quarterly, 77*(1), 65–88. https://doi.org/10.1177/2329490613511493

Koerber, A., & Graham, H. (2017). Theorizing the value of English proficiency in cross-cultural rhetorics of health and medicine: A qualitative study. *Journal of Business and Technical Communication, 31*(1), 63–93. https://doi.org/10.1177/1050651916667533

Kohn, L. (2015). How professional writing pedagogy and university-workplace partnerships can shape the mentoring of workplace writing. *Journal of Technical Writing & Communication, 45*(2), 166–188. https://doi-org.libe2.lib.ttu.edu/10.1177/0047281615569484

Kryder, L. (1995, Spring). Reconciling writing in academic and workplace settings. *Writing on the Edge, 6*(2). Retrieved from https://www.jstor.org/stable/43156970

Lamar Reinsch, N., & Gardner, J. A. (2014). Do communication abilities affect promotion decisions? Some data from the C-suite. *Journal of Business and Technical Communication, 28*(1), 31–57. https://doi.org/10.1177/1050651913502357

Lanier, C. R. (2009). Creating editorial authority through technological innovation. *Journal of Technical Writing & Communication, 39*(4), 467–479. https://doi-org.lib-e2.lib.ttu.edu/10.2190/TW.39.4.h

Lee, M. F., & Mehlenbacher, B. (2000, November). Technical writer/subject-matter expert interaction: The writer's perspective, the organizational challenge. *Technical Communication, 47*(4). Retrieved from https://www.jstor.org/stable/43748973

Lentz, P. (2013). MBA students' workplace writing: Implications for business writing pedagogy and workplace practice. *Business Communication Quarterly, 76*(4), 474–490. https://doi.org/10.1177/1080569913507479

Lerner, N. (2014). The unpromising present of writing center studies: Author and citation patterns in *The Writing Center Journal*, 1980 to 2009. *The Writing Center Journal, 34*(1), 67–102.

Lucas, K., & Rawlins, J. D. (2015). The competency pivot: Introducing a revised approach to the business communication curriculum. *Business and Professional Communication Quarterly, 78*(2), 167–193. https://doi.org/10.1177/2329490615576071

Mabrito, M. (1999, September). From workplace to classroom: Teaching professional writing. *Business Communication Quarterly, 62*(3), 101–105.

Machili, I., Angouri, J., & Harwood, N. (2019). 'The snowball of emails we deal with': CCing in multinational companies. *Business and Professional Communication Quarterly, 82*(1), 5–37. https://doi.org/10.1177/2329490618815700

Mackiewicz, J. (2012). Relying on writing consultants: The design of a WID program for a college of business. *Journal of Business and Technical Communication, 26*(2), 229–258. https://doi.org/10.1177/1050651911429924

Mackiewicz, J. (2014). Motivating quality: The impact of amateur editors' suggestions on user generated content at epinions.com. *Journal of Business and Technical Communication, 28*(4), 419–446. https://doi.org/10.1177/1050651914535930

Mallette, J. C. (2017). Writing and women's retention in engineering. *Journal of Business and Technical Communication, 31*(4), 417–442. https://doi.org/10.1177/1050651917713253

Marlow, S. L., Lacerenza, C. N., & Iwig, C. (2018). The influence of textual cues on first impressions of an email sender. *Business and Professional Communication Quarterly, 81*(2), 149–166. https://doi.org/10.1177/2329490617723115

McCloskey, D. N. (1998). *The rhetoric of economics* (2nd ed.). Madison: The University of Wisconsin Press.

McNamara, D. S., Crossley, S. A., & McCarthy, P. M. (2010). Linguistic features of writing quality. *Written Communication, 27*(1), 57–86. https://doi.org/10.1177/0741088309351547

Miller, C. (1979). A humanistic rationale for technical writing. *College English, 40*(6), 610–617.

Moshiri, F., & Cardon, P. (2014). The state of business communication classes: A national survey. *Business and Professional Communication Quarterly, 77*(3), 312–329. https://doi.org/10.1177/2329490614538489

North, S. M. (1984, September). The idea of a writing center. *College English, 46*(5), 433–446.

Omilion-Hodges, L. M., & Sugg, C. E. (2019). Millennials' view and expectations regarding the communicative and relational behaviors of leaders: Exploring young adults' talk about work. *Business and Professional Communication Quarterly, 82*(1), 74–100. https://doi.org/10.1177/2329490618808043

Ore, E. (2017). Pushback: A pedagogy of care. *Pedagogy: Critical Approaches to Teaching Literature, Language, Composition, and Culture, 17*(1), 9–33.

Ortiz, L. A., Region-Sebest, M., & MacDermott, C. (2016). Employer perceptions of oral communication competencies most valued in new hires as a factor in company success. *Business and Professional Communication Quarterly, 79*(3), 317–330. https://doi.org/10.1177/2329490615624108

Perdue, S. W., & Driscoll, D. L. (2017). Context matters: Centering writing center administrators' institutional status and scholarly identity. *Writing Center Journal, 36*(1), 185–214.

Quick, C. (2012). From the workplace to academia: Nontraditional students and the relevance of workplace experience in technical writing pedagogy. *Technical Communication Quarterly, 21*(3), 230–250. https://doi-org.lib-e2.lib.ttu.edu/10.1080/1057 2252.2012.666639

Rentz, K. C. (2015). Beyond the generational stereotypes: A study of U.S. Generation Y employees in context. *Business and Professional Communication Quarterly, 78*(2), 136– 166. https://doi.org/10.1177/2329490615576183

Rice-Bailey, T. (2016). The role and value of technical communicators: Technical communicators and subject matter experts weigh in. *Technical Communication Quarterly, 25*(4), 230–243. https://doi-org.lib-e2.lib.ttu.edu/10.1080/10572252.2016.1221140

Riley, T. (1994). The unpromising future of writing centers. *The Writing Center Journal, 15*(1), 20–34. Retrieved from http://www.jstor.org/stable/43442607

Salas, E., Tannenbaum, S. I., Kraiger, K., & Smith-Jentsch, K. A. (2012). The science of training and development in organizations: What matters in practice. *Psychological Science in the Public Interest, 13*(2). Retrieved from https://www.jstor.org/stable/23484697

Salem, L. (2014). Opportunity and transformation: How writing centers are positioned in the political landscape of higher education in the United States. *Writing Center Journal, 34*(1), 15–43.

Smart, G. (1999, July). Storytelling in a central bank: The role of narrative in the creation and use of specialized economic knowledge. *Journal of Business and Technical Communication, 13*(3), 249–273.

Sollitto, M., & Cranmer, G. A. (2019). The relationship between aggressive communication traits and organizational assimilation. *International Journal of Business Communication, 56*(2), 278–296. https://doi-org.lib-e2.lib.ttu.edu/10.1177/2329488415613339

Spinuzzi, C. (2010). Secret sauce and snake oil: Writing monthly reports in a highly contingent environment. *Written Communication, 27*(4), 363–409.

Steiner, D. G. (2011). The communication habits of engineers: A study of how compositional style and time affect the production of oral and written communication of engineers. *Journal of Technical Writing & Communication, 41*(1), 33–58. https:// doi-org.lib-e2.lib.ttu.edu/10.2190/TW.41.1.c

Taylor, S. S. (2011). "I really don't know what he meant by that": How well do engineering students understand teachers' comments on their writing? *Technical Communication Quarterly, 20*(2), 139–166. https://doi-org.lib-e2.lib.ttu.edu/10.1080/10572 252.2011.548762

Trimbur, J. (2010). Multiliteracies, social futures, and writing centers. *Writing Center Journal, 30*(1), 88–91.

U.S. Government Accountability Office. (2019). What GAO does. Retrieved from https://www.gao.gov/about/what-gao-does/.

Van Der Steen, S., Samuelson, D., & Thomson, J. M. (2017). The effect of keyboard-based word processing on students with different working memory capacity during the process of academic writing. *Written Communication, 34*(3), 280–305. https://doi.org/10.1177/0741088317714232

Vaughn, E. (2020, September 14). Redesigning the office for the next 100-year flu (yes, it's coming). *NPR.* Retrieved from https://www.npr.org/sections/ health-shots/2020/09/14/909805060/redesigning-the-office-to-maximize-health

Waddell, A., & Pio, E. (2015). The influence of senior leaders on organisational learning: Insights from the employees' perspectives. *Management Learning, 46*(4), 461–478.

Wang, J. (2010). Convergence in the rhetorical pattern of directness and indirectness in Chinese and U.S. business letters. *Journal of Business and Technical Communication, 24*(1), 91–120. https://doi.org/10.1177/1050651909346933

Wiggins, G. (2009, May). EJ in focus: Real-world writing: Making purpose and audience matter. *The English Journal, 98*(5). Retrieved from https://www.jstor.org/ stable/40503292

Wolfe, J. (2009). How technical communication textbooks fail engineering students. *Technical Communication Quarterly, 18*(4), 351–375. https://doi-org.libe2.lib.ttu. edu/10.1080/10572250903149662

Yates, J., Orlikowski, W. J., & Okamura, K. (1999). Explicit and implicit structuring of genres in electronic communication: Reinforcement and change of social interaction. *Organization Science, 10*(1), 83–103.

Yu, H. (2010). Bring workplace assessment into business communication classrooms: A proposal to better prepare students for professional workplaces. *Business and Professional Communication Quarterly, 73*(1), 21–39. https://journals-sagepub-com.libe2.lib. ttu.edu/doi/pdf/10.1177/1080569909357783

Part 2

Building the Workplace Writing Center

3 Pitching and Ensuring a Successful Model

First, let me elaborate on the approaches and values I've applied within the writing centers I've launched. Borrowing this language may be helpful as you conceive of what services and approaches will be most helpful to your own workplace.

Approaches and Values for Your Pitch

Establishing an Ideal Writing Support Structure

Like most writing centers, a workplace writing center should be designed to facilitate writers' learning and to gain their trust. If your writing center will offer workshops, be sure to allow time for group work, individual work, and questions; encourage participants to interact and to weigh in on what they'd like to focus on. Whenever possible, include [appropriate redacted] examples from real documents, and align training as closely as possible to their everyday reality, which encourages their motivation to learn (Salas, Tannenbaum, Kraiger, & Smith-Jentsch, 2012). Be sure to avoid lecture-style classroom trainings and related vocabulary. I have always preferred the term *consultant* to other alternatives, in part because terms like *teacher* can become "problematic in an environment where the teacher cannot profess to have detailed understanding of the knowledge, skills, and work practices of individual worksite" (Castleton, 2002, p. 561). Mimicking a school environment too closely can also perpetuate hierarchies in the workplace, further dividing those at different levels (Castleton, 2002; Clayson, 2018). Holding confidential conferences also helps to make writers more comfortable and identify individual goals and needs among staff (Askov, 1993, p. 550).

Working alongside and collaboratively with writers is vital. Writing center staff and leadership should have experience in tutoring and consulting, as well as a strong background in rhetoric, writing, or a related field. Though consultants need not share subject expertise with writers (Luo & Hyland, 2017), having the writing center embedded within the workplace helps to expose consultants to subject matter on a day-to-day basis (Mackiewicz, 2012). But most significant is the ability of consultants to immerse themselves in the writers' world, asking questions to understand writers' "current reality

DOI: 10.4324/9781003212959-6

and vision" (Stowers & Barker, 2010, p. 364). Interactions can take place with writers in many ways outside of document revision and writing consultations. Consultants can take advantage of the kinds of social practices that Spinuzzi describes as being "as minor as eating breakfast taccos together, as subtle as checking on someone's availability by seeing if they are logged into IM" (2010, p. 393). This is where important work happens, where trust and relationships are built; consultants should be just as much a part of the workplace culture as the writers are (Kohn, 2015, p. 184).

Easing the Transition for New Employees to the Workplace

An appealing benefit for many workplaces will be a writing center's ability to help new employees communicate efficiently in a particular context. Given the importance that employees ascribe to strong writing skills, it's surprising that more organizations don't provide sustainable writing instruction and support for new employees—especially young professionals and employees who have backgrounds in a different industry. One common form of instruction that *is* provided by some workplaces is "document modeling", where a writer may be given past documents to follow as a guide, but otherwise receives "little on-the-job training to help them develop as writers" (Mabrito, 1997, p. 68). These models may become crutches that writers use long past their effectiveness; at past workplaces, I found that writers would continue following older, outdated models and/or would fail to tailor them to each specific rhetorical situation.

Beyond saving time and money, offering writing "feedback aligns workplace behavior with the overall goals of a team or an organization" (Harms & Roebuck, 2010, p. 413). In learning how to communicate in the voice of the organization, writers don't just strengthen their writing skills, but they also learn how to participate in organizational culture. Writing centers can help support new employees learning to deal with some oft-cited writing challenges, including preferences for personal styles, teams being physically separated within different buildings, or multiple people accessing and editing a document at once (Colen & Petelin, 2004). But one of the greatest challenges for new employees remains adapting to writing outside of a classroom, which usually allows for a quiet, uninterrupted environment (Steiner, 2011). Some employees put off writing until the last minute because they loathe the task (Steiner, 2011); one study even found that half of their workforce reported "apprehension, reluctance, and dread" when writing (Aldrich, 1982, p. 287). Though students learn that writing is important in the workplace, many underestimate the sheer amount of writing they'll need to do on the job (Barnett, 2012; Steiner, 2011).

Assisting with Difficult Workplace Genres and Situations

When I was a student tutor in different university writing centers, I worked with many students on documents that were highly sensitive or personal to them. But the types of high-stakes writing that come with workplace situations is treacherous in an entirely different way (and with a much wider impact). It can be difficult enough for employees to try to learn to write with the voice of an organization, but they also face the fact that readers tend to react more severely to an organization's voice than to a supervisor's (Bisel & Messersmith, 2012, p. 434). When I have guided writers through writing reports that deliver bad news, we are both intuitively and painfully aware of this unique challenge as we borrow the voice of authority. Writing generated on behalf of an organization, specifically that which delivers difficult news, has become increasingly more challenging. Writers need to navigate layoff memos in the age of social media (DuFrene & Lehman, 2014), deliver press releases that will reach multiple levels of stakeholders (Lehtimäki, Kujala, & Heikkinen, 2011, p. 447), or notify millions of clients about a data breach (Veltsos, 2012, p. 203). Though it can be tempting to bury bad news in a lengthy memo or to avoid communication altogether, it's critical for writers—especially those in positions of power—to be clear and to communicate openly in order to establish trust and maintain morale, particularly in times of organizational change (DuFrene & Lehman, 2014).

Pitching the Workplace Writing Center

Organization's Buy-In

Although anyone interested in creating a workplace writing center now has an existing (and so far, successful) model to point to, ensuring the organization's buy-in is a critical first step. One way to pitch a workplace writing center as a worthwhile investment is to research the amount of funds the organization currently allocates toward writing training and/or improving writing. If the organization has been spending large sums on hiring an outside professional to teach occasional workshops—as many workplaces do—it becomes easier to lay out a case for why ongoing support from a writing center would be a wiser investment. There is also an abundance of research supporting the fact that writing training and support can increase work productivity, thus saving organizations money over time (Catanio & Catanio, 2010, p. 95). Some organizations may also be better positioned to develop a writing center based on their own mission and vision. In my experience, working with organizations that value professional development and ongoing training has been a key component of success.

Workplaces may also reap a wide range of benefits by committing to improving effective communication within their ranks. Effective communication has been shown as "significantly related to job satisfaction, motivation, and organizational commitment" (Mikkelson, York, & Arritola, 2015, p. 347). And when employees receive clear expectations from managers, they tend to be more motivated to meet these goals (p. 349). Though some organizations may be tempted to use a writing center to "fix" less experienced or tenured employees, the truth is that it is a resource that can benefit the organization at and between each level.

Culture Shifts

Implementing a successful workplace writing center involves facilitating a shift in attitudes, beliefs, and even culture within an organization. With employees arriving from many different educational, career, and life backgrounds, it's important for any efficient organization to encourage a cohesive, clear approach to communication. Even if an organization provides the support necessary for a writing center, it should be made clear that results will not appear overnight—in my experience, it's taken closer to six months to see signs of improvement. Framing writing center-related changes as process improvement may help encourage a longer-term, open-minded approach (Lanier, 2009, p. 476).

There will absolutely be some resistance when a new workplace writing center is introduced. Writers may see this new resource as a dismantling of *the old way of doing things.* In many workplaces, "communication habits and the genres resulting from those habits have become entrenched routines that continually reaffirm the purpose and form of the established communication process"; challenging these can "represent a significant organizational intervention" (Suchan, 2014, p. 453). And with any major organizational change, employees can find themselves fearing the unknown and feeling threatened as the rules they knew well begin to unravel or waver (Faber, 2002, p. 66). Though I have tried to make workplace writers feel *more* in control by stressing their agency in new revision processes, some were still anxious about my motives and how they may be penalized for compliance (or noncompliance).

Anticipating resistance and anxiety is crucial, but there are further steps that you can take to help ease the introduction of a workplace writing center into a new space. Major changes are better managed with clear and continual communication with all levels of the organization. Such communication may include "[e]xplaining the process accurately and honestly, highlighting its value for the future, and rewarding subordinates for their goal-directed behaviors" (Hartge, Callahan, & King, 2019, p. 115). Similarly, I have encouraged managers to explain to their staff why the writing center is being created, and to encourage writers to use these resources.

Another way I have helped employees to embrace changes is by keeping writing center consultations and services voluntary, whenever possible. Not only is forcing someone to have a positive learning experience typically a futile endeavor, but keeping people from having any choice over their initial engagement can leave them feeling like "a constant victim of external circumstances" (Levy, 2017, p. 66). Employees may also adapt to these changes more positively if they are allowed to have a voice in the implementation. Culture change within an organization begins with a narrative that the organization wants to tell, and allowing individual units or employees to contribute to this narrative can be helpful (Dulek, 2015).

The narratives that drive culture change do not necessarily have to be built from scratch. All workplaces are guided by some kind of mission, vision, purpose, or philosophy, whether they strive for efficiency, profit, or a greater humanitarian good. If culture change can be tied to the goals that underscore the organization's operations, it can encourage employees and supervisors to buy in to it. Tying the writing center's goals to the organization's mission can also help establish the writing center as a more valuable resource. In the case of technical communicators, those who "consistently identify and solve important corporate problems and who develop innovations that positively impact the corporation's bottom line" are more highly valued (Hailey, Cox, & Loader, 2010, p. 139). In workplace writing consultations, I have spoken about how my mission contributes directly to the organization's mission. I point to how important clarity and succinctness are in different documents; if messages become lost in dense, disorganized prose, so too is the value of our work.

Manager Support

No matter how much authority you are given when you begin to lead a workplace writing center, writers are almost always going to defer to their managers' advice and preferences. For this reason, it is critical to ensure management's buy-in early on in the process of introducing a writing center. If writers understand that managers will be holding them accountable for the quality of their writing, they are more likely to put forth the effort to utilize the writing center. Knowing that managers may consider writing quality in performance reviews and/or when recommending individuals for promotion is another powerful motivating factor for employees (Lentz, 2013, p. 487). This is not to say that withholding promotions from struggling writers is a threat to wield. Rather, managers can let employees know that their efforts to improve writing skills will not go unnoticed or unappreciated. In my own experience—through surveys—writers underestimated the weight that managers put in writing skills when considering who should earn a promotion.

Though writing consultations should be kept as voluntary as possible, I have led plenty of workshops that managers have designated as mandatory for their teams. Because attending a one-time workshop is a limited commitment for employees, I generally do not intervene if managers want to mandate attendance. It is rare that I design workshops to be longer than two hours, as this is a sufficient amount of time for participants to remain alert and engaged, pick up a few worthwhile tips, and maintain an interest in other ongoing support available through the writing center. Participant feedback has consistently been much more positive for two-hour workshops rather than four- or six-hour workshops. If I am traveling to lead workshops at different workplace sites, I try to offer the same workshop twice (once in the morning, once in the afternoon) in order to accommodate different schedules. It's imperative that managers make the same effort to keep these workshops and resources easily accessible. Managers should encourage their teams to take advantages of these resources, as well as allow flexibility in their team's scheduling so that they can easily attend workshops when offered (Catanio & Catanio, 2010). Providing this ongoing support for learning and development can help "alleviate burn-out, build trust, and most importantly, enhance individual competencies that will improve team performance, and in effect, influence new learning in the organization" (p. 86).

Perhaps the most powerful way that managers can express their support for the writing center is by attending workshops or scheduling one-on-one consultations themselves. Employees are more likely to embrace change if they see their leaders actively taking part in the change themselves, particularly if this behavior is repeated and clearly communicated over time (Hartge et al., 2019, p. 112). I've witnessed this any time a manager makes the effort to attend their own one-on-one writing consultation before recommending the service to their team. The experience allowed the manager to not only see the benefits for themselves but also provide accurate information to their team about what this experience would be like.

Summary

One of the most important things you can do as you begin to set up a workplace writing center is to ensure the full support of leadership throughout the organization. Writing centers in any context are frequently mistaken for editorial "fix-it shops", imbued with the power to perfect any document instantly. It is important that stakeholders see the writing center as a long-term investment that builds skills over time: Patience and vocal support are imperative.

Writers are more likely to use the writing center—and to have a positive, meaningful experience—when they are invited to do so voluntarily. Writing centers should be seen as a resource that is allied with writers, helping them to adapt to workplace culture and language. It should never feel punitive or remedial; rather, it should feel like a secret weapon that helps them to thrive in their environment.

Inviting writers, managers, and executive leadership to take part in the early development of the workplace writing center is an excellent way to begin building trust. This involvement will also help you to create a writing center that is well suited to the particular context, and that will drive meaningful results. The following chapter will provide more detail about how to map the workplace and determine just where your workplace writing center will best fit in.

References

Aldrich, P. G. (1982). Adult writers: Some reasons for ineffective writing on the job. *College Composition and Communication, 33*(3), 284–287.

Askov, E. N. (1993). Approaches to assessment in workplace literacy programs: Meeting the needs of all the clients. *Journal of Reading, 36*(7), 550–554.

Barnett, K. (2012). Student interns' socially constructed work realities: Narrowing the work expectation-reality gap. *Business Communication Quarterly, 75*(3), 271–290. https://doi.org/10.1177/1080569912441360

Bisel, R. S., & Messersmith, A. S. (2012). Organizational and supervisory apology effectiveness: Apology giving in work settings. *Business Communication Quarterly, 75*(4), 425–448. https://doi.org/10.1177/1080569912461171

Castleton, G. (2002, April). Workplace literacy as a contested site of educational activity. *Journal of Adolescent & Adult Literacy, 45*(7). Retrieved from https://www.jstor.org/stable/40012240.

Catanio, J. T., & Catanio, T. L. (2010). The effects of integrating on-going training for technical documentation teams. *Journal of Technical Writing & Communication, 40*(1), 77–97. https://doi-org.libe2.lib.ttu.edu/10.2190/TW.40.1.e

Clayson, A. (2018). Distributed cognition and embodiment in text planning: A situated study of collaborative writing in the workplace. *Written Communication, 35*(2), 155–181. https://doi.org/10.1177/0741088317753348

Colen, K., & Petelin, R. (2004). Challenges in collaborative writing in the contemporary corporation. *Corporate Communications, 9*(2), 136–145.

DuFrene, D. D., & Lehman, C. M. (2014). Navigating change: Employee communication in times of instability. *Business and Professional Communication Quarterly, 77*(4), 443–452. https://doi.org/10.1177/2329490614544736

Dulek, R. E. (2015). Instituting cultural change at a major organization: A case study. *Business and Professional Communication Quarterly, 78*(2), 231–243. https://doi.org/10.1177/2329490614554991

Faber, B. D. (2002). *Community action and organizational change: Image, narrative, identity.* (1st ed.). Carbondale: Southern Illinois University Press.

Hailey, D., Cox, M., & Loader, E. (2010). Relationship between innovation and professional communication in the "creative" economy. *Journal of Technical Writing & Communication, 40*(2), 125–141. https://doi-org.lib-e2.lib.ttu.edu/10.2190/TW.40.2.b

Harms, P. L., & Roebuck, D. B. (2010). Teaching the art and craft of giving and receiving feedback. *Business and Professional Communication Quarterly, 73*(4), 413–431. https://journalssagepub-com.lib-e2.lib.ttu.edu/doi/pdf/10.1177/1080569910385565

Hartge, T., Callahan, T., & King, C. (2019). Leaders' behaviors during radical change processes: Subordinates' perceptions of how well leader behaviors communicate change. *International Journal of Business Communication, 56*(1), 100–121. https://doi-org.lib-e2.lib.ttu.edu/10.1177/2329488415605061

Kohn, L. (2015). How professional writing pedagogy and university-workplace partnerships can shape the mentoring of workplace writing. *Journal of Technical Writing & Communication, 45*(2), 166–188. https://doi-org.libe2.lib.ttu.edu/10.1177/0047281615569484

Lanier, C. R. (2009). Creating editorial authority through technological innovation. *Journal of Technical Writing & Communication, 39*(4), 467–479. https://doi-org.lib-e2.lib.ttu.edu/10.2190/TW.39.4.h

Lehtimäki, H., Kujala, J., & Heikkinen, A. (2011). Corporate responsibility in communication: Empirical analysis of press releases in a conflict. *Business Communication Quarterly, 74*(4), 432–449. https://doi.org/10.1177/1080569911424203

Lentz, P. (2013). MBA students' workplace writing: Implications for business writing pedagogy and workplace practice. *Business Communication Quarterly, 76*(4), 474–490. https://doi.org/10.1177/1080569913507479

Levy, A. (2017). *Mastering organizational change: Theory and practice.* [Independently published].

Luo, N., & Hyland, K. (2017). Intervention and revision: Expertise and interaction in text mediation. *Written Communication, 34*(4), 414–440. https://doi.org/10.1177/0741088317722944

Mabrito, M. (1997). Writing on the front line: A study of workplace writing. *Business Communication Quarterly, 60*(3), 58–70.

Mackiewicz, J. (2012). Relying on writing consultants: The design of a WID program for a college of business. *Journal of Business and Technical Communication, 26*(2), 229–258. https://doi.org/10.1177/1050651911429924

Mikkelson, A. C., York, J. A., & Arritola, J. (2015). Communication competence, leadership behaviors, and employee outcomes in supervisor-employee relationships. *Business and Professional Communication Quarterly, 78*(3), 336–354. https://doi.org/10.1177/2329490615588542

Salas, E., Tannenbaum, S. I., Kraiger, K., & Smith-Jentsch, K. A. (2012). The science of training and development in organizations: What matters in practice. *Psychological Science in the Public Interest, 13*(2). Retrieved from https://www.jstor.org/stable/23484697

Spinuzzi, C. (2010). Secret sauce and snake oil: Writing monthly reports in a highly contingent environment. *Written Communication, 27*(4), 363–409.

Steiner, D. G. (2011). The communication habits of engineers: A study of how compositional style and time affect the production of oral and written communication of engineers. *Journal of Technical Writing & Communication, 41*(1), 33–58. https://doi-org.lib-e2.lib.ttu.edu/10.2190/TW.41.1.c

Stowers, R. H., & Barker, R. T. (2010). The coaching and mentoring process: The obvious knowledge and skill set for organizational communication professors. *Journal of Technical Writing & Communication, 40*(3), 363–371. https://doi-org.lib-e2.lib.ttu.edu/10.2190/TW.40.3.g

Suchan, J. (2014). Gauging openness to written communication change: The predictive power of metaphor. *Journal of Business and Technical Communication, 28*(4), 447–476. https://doi.org/10.1177/1050651914536187

Veltsos, J. R. (2012). An analysis of data breach notifications as negative news. *Business Communication Quarterly, 75*(2), 192–207. https://doi.org/10.1177/1080569912443081

4 Mapping the Workplace

Every workplace looks different, so every workplace writing center will need to take a slightly different approach. Mapping out your workplace is a key early step to setting up a successful writing center that works within, not against, existing workplace dynamics. This chapter will guide you through considering various aspects of your workplace, and how to collect relevant data.

Getting Started

Departments and Pilots

First, consider the size of your workplace. You can consult organizational charts if they are listed on a workplace's internal site, or you can reach out to a supervisor who can help you with this information. If you are at a smaller workplace with fewer employees, gathering information may be a simple step. But workplace writing centers are more likely to find success within larger organizations with bigger budgets and more employees. Larger workplaces can have more complicated structures, particularly if you are working with a government agency, a national nonprofit, or a corporation with global offices or partners.

For larger workplace organizations, you may want to ask the following.

- How does your organization fit into a larger structure? Is there a central site with higher authority than the site you are at?
- Do other branches of your workplace site exist, and if so, will you be expected to offer them support as well? If your workplace exists in multiple branches/sites, are the writing expectations drastically different between them?
- How many departments exist within your workplace? How do the sizes of these departments compare? In what department will the writing center be contained, and how might this impact access to resources, budgeting, and exposure to other departments?
- What will be the writing center's capacity for expansion? If your resource becomes well established, will you be able to hire an intern and/or part-time or full-time staff? What does this process look like?

DOI: 10.4324/9781003212959-7

It may be wise to begin with a pilot, especially if you are at a larger organization. In my own experience, I have launched workplace writing centers within a particular department, and I have extended services on a rolling basis to different units within that first department. This phased approach has kept our consultants from becoming too overwhelmed by demand. It also allows for the collection of positive testimonials before marketing services more widely beyond your pilot audience.

You are likely to know early on where your advocates are located within the workplace. Perhaps it is within a unit that first expressed the need for writing improvement. It may be a high-priority area or the unit that writes the most frequently. It may simply be the unit that had the budget to house the writing center. But if you do not know where you should pilot your writing center within the workplace, consider asking leadership the following questions about the different departments or units within the workplace.

- Where is writing the most crucial component of the job?
- What (or where) are the high-priority objectives that depend on clear messaging?
- Which teams are facing the most challenges related to their writing?
- Which teams would be most receptive to writing resources?
- Where could we find a strong writing center advocate who could encourage their team to use its resources?

A workplace that has invested in the creation of a workplace writing center is likely to already have these areas of focus in mind. But if less clear guidance is available to you, then you may consider creating a survey for writers and/or identifying a sponsor who can help you determine areas of focus.

Surveys and Sponsors

If you have the opportunity to pilot a workplace writing center within a smaller workplace—*or* if you are not given much direction from leadership in a larger workplace—you may find it helpful to administer a survey to the writers who may (or may not) use the writing center.

More detail on creating a needs assessment can be found in Chapter 7, and more on designing and distributing surveys can be found in Chapter 9. A simple set of Likert scale questions can help you get a feel for which writers or teams of writers may make a good starting point as a pilot audience. For example, you could ask respondents whether they "strongly disagree", "disagree", "agree", or "strongly agree" with the following statements.

- One of my current goals is to improve my writing.
- I would be willing to work with a writing coach to improve my skills.
- I would be willing to attend a short writing workshop.
- I believe writing is an important part of my job.

- I am confident in the quality of my writing.
- I believe I receive adequate feedback on my writing.

Responses to these questions may reveal particular teams or areas that would be grateful for additional support—or even those who do not see writing as a priority, and who likely would not make a good starting point for a pilot.

Determining a sponsor for the writing center can also help you to identify a pilot location (and/or where to expand as your writing center grows). An ideal sponsor is someone who will spread the word about the writing center and who understands the writing center's mission and purpose. They will communicate with and across teams to encourage writing center use; ideally, they will be willing to use the service themselves and to share their experience with others. Having a respectable leader vocally support the writing center has been, in my experience, one of the best ways to encourage people to make use of new resources and services.

Common Workplace Writing Issues

Some of the challenges facing workplace writers are the same that plague students, while others are unique to a workplace environment. The following categories—organization, support and analysis, tone, style, clarity, and grammar and proofreading—will guide you through some common workplace writing issues to expect. These six categories may also help you to organize your conversations with managers and staff as you learn more about the unique writing style in your workplace.

Organization

I look at *organization* as the bones of a written piece—if they're not in place, the rest won't be enough for the piece to stand on its own. Many American students learn, at some point during their primary or secondary schooling, that they can use the "sandwich method"[1] to deliver difficult news; this can be disastrous when trying to gain an audience's trust and understanding (French & Holden, 2012, p. 217). I personally learned the "Tootsie roll" method of organizing a paper, wherein you're encouraged to begin with broad, sweeping generalizations, and then narrow your ideas to a more focused main point. This approach is … a truly terrible way to communicate in the real world, or at least outside of academia. Usually when I open the organization-focused portion of my writing workshops, I share the story of how I learned about one tactic that has become particularly popular among my coworkers: BLUF, or *bottom line up front*. When I was in college (and majoring in creative writing), I dated an ROTC cadet who would occasionally ask me to check his write-ups for errors before he turned them in. I would often suggest adding details here and there to make them more interesting, at which point he reminded me that no one cares about pleasing details when you're trying to execute military orders.

Your workplace's writing may have less dire circumstances than front-line military orders, but you will still be able to identify serious ramifications for the audiences at hand. Organization-wise, good workplace writing is that which prioritizes the main points and clearly leads readers between them.

When working with a writer who struggles with organization, it can help to identify what led them to make the writing choices they made. Sometimes, poor organization results from a writer's failure to plan out an argument or message in advance. Or it could be the product of an inefficient system of revision, which may extend well beyond them. In many workplaces, report review processes include too many different levels, with each level of supervisor "simply add[ing] bits and pieces of information without integrating them into a coherent report" (Mabrito, 1997, p. 63). This common practice can lead to buried or misunderstood information, and can even perpetuate poor writing practices if later writers look to these reports as a model.

Support and Analysis

Another crucial element in strong workplace writing is knowing how much detail to include to support your main point(s). Although workplace writing consultants should not weigh in too directly on the technical ways writers choose to back up their findings, they can point out where readers may have lingering questions. Less-experienced workplace writers may provide an embarrassment of support for their points as a way of proving themselves in a new context. This can be particularly troublesome when multiple writers are collaborating on a longer report; writers may feel pressured to write the same amount as their colleagues, when the reader would actually benefit from increased detail in urgent sections of the report and fewer details elsewhere. An abundance of information can also be overwhelming for readers in general (Jones, McDavid, Derthick, Dowell, & Spyridakis, 2012). At the same time, some writers go too far in the opposite direction and do not provide adequate support for difficult messages or for findings that may be contested by readers. When I reach the support and analysis portion of my writing workshops, I often ask writers about their strategies for determining how much support is appropriate. One answer that I will never forget was from a young woman in Boston: "A professor once told me that writing should be like a skirt: long enough to cover the basics, but short enough to keep it…interesting". This is not advice that I've chosen to add in any of my workplace writing guides, as it's not a conversation I'd like to have with Human Resources, but it did make for lively conversation throughout the rest of the workshop.

While the question of adequate and/or appropriate levels of support comes up commonly in academic writing center sessions, the question can be trickier in the workplace. High-stakes deliverables may be read by multiple audiences, each with a different level of content familiarity and understanding. It is important to consider who primary audiences are, as well as what vehicles may exist for adding additional support (e.g., footnotes, supplementary documents, hyperlinks). Workplace documents don't typically exist in a vacuum, either—they're often follow-ups to previous reports or are part of an ongoing project with many more written pieces. Thinking through how these documents may reference one another and how accessible they may be to various readers is important, too. Another consideration is document lifespan and whether the writer needs to be careful about how much detail is being recorded.

Tone

So much of workplace writing shapes relationships with stakeholders, and tone is one of the most impactful writing elements. Writers are tasked with managing trust and credibility with readers (Walton, 2013, p. 100) and to ensure that messages are received as positively as possible (Jones et al., 2012, p. 358). Though it's always important to use a respectful tone with readers, severity of tone may vary based on the message being communicated and the audience's past responsiveness.

Writers who are newer to an organization or who are naturally less assertive tend to make the tone of their writing too gentle. Those who are new to a workplace or to the workforce in general "have no confidants within the group to reduce social distance", and thus may "couch their statements with negative politeness strategies (most commonly, apologies, hedges, and conversational indirectness) to attempt to mitigate the threat to the hearer's face" (Friess, 2013, p. 313). This can be a dangerous strategy in workplace writing—if writers are too polite and indirect when delivering difficult messages, readers are liable to underestimate the gravity of findings or bottom lines. It's also possible for writers to undermine their own or the organization's authority by sounding as if they lack confidence in their assertions.

At the same time, using too harsh of a tone can be just as damaging to rapport with readers. Some writers believe that "[s]trong, harsh, forceful language...is necessary to defend themselves and their departments, to protect their organizations legally, to move readers to action, or to achieve other goals" (Jameson, 2009, p. 334). There is certainly a time and place for using a firm tone, but more assertive writers tend to overuse it. When a tone is harsher than necessary, readers may be insulted and inadvertently miss or deliberately ignore our primary message. One of my mentors has likened this to scolding a child for getting a B on an exam because they have, in the past, scored higher. If writers are too harsh in evaluative writing tasks, they may undermine the value of what was done well, and thus provide no incentive for improved performance in the future.

Style

Style is one of the trickiest elements to consider because it can vary drastically by context and/or writing task. I think of workplace style as a sort of written dialect that writers need to learn in order to communicate success-fully within an organization and/or communicate through the voice of an organization. Some style features may come from standards and guidance already implemented in your workplace, but others may be more nuanced—in which case, you may be tasked with describing and teaching this style to less experienced writers. In many workplaces, employees are tasked with the challenge of using their own voices, but only as far as they "fit well with the company's brand, goals, and identity" (Weber, 2013, p. 300). Your workplace's distinct style will likely include both minor features, such as the number of decimals used to communicate certain technical measurements, and major features, such as when to reference a standard-language disclaimer in a foot-note or slide. Newer employees tend to struggle more with style than their more seasoned counterparts do, as style knowledge comes with on-the-job experience and practice.

Clarity

In recent years, there have been a number of initiatives to make writing clearer and more transparent in various industries. The Plain Writing Act of 2010 requires US federal agencies to improve their communications so that they can be easily understood by the public (Greer, 2012). Whether or not your organization formally falls under this Act, it's an important movement toward transparency that should be considered. Efforts toward clearer writing can increase the public's trust and understanding, as well as save money for public agencies (Jones et al., 2012, pp. 332–335). But clarity doesn't come easily to most writers. As workplace writing guru Josh Bern-off eloquently puts it: "In high school, you learned to write verbose prose to fool teachers into believing you knew what you were talking about. Those teachers taught you that bullshitting was effective" (Bernoff, 2016, p. 4). Unfortunately, bullshitting is not effective in the real world—or at the very least, it's not sustainably effective. Bernoff argues that students learn "that avoiding risk [is] paramount" and that "[c]larity can be dan-gerous because people who read what you wrote might disagree with it" (2016, p. 4).

It's true that if we are being clear in our writing, we have to be ready to defend our points and to lead readers to acceptance and understanding of our message. But often, writers need some encouragement to embrace the clarity and transparency that can leave them feeling exposed. They also, at times, need to be reminded to empathize with readers and their needs. This chal-lenge may be especially difficult for those with high levels of specialization and technical expertise—it's easy to lose sight of where audiences may need additional clarification and/or where they may need less technical language in general. A writing center consultant, of course, is an excellent support for these reader-related concerns.

Grammar and Proofreading

When most writers come to a writing center for the first time, they typically believe the center exists to proofread their pieces and to make surface-level revisions. Though the workplace writing centers I've led and advised will look for surface-level grammatical, spelling, and mechanical errors, they only do so when (1) the writer explicitly asks for this type of review, especially if they are a nonnative English speaker (NNES) or (2) the writer demonstrates a strong grasp on all other aspects of the writing (e.g., organization, support/analysis, tone, style, clarity). This approach grew partly out of the fact that grammar is a relatively easy back-end fix for our writing consultants. If consultants have a formal role in review processes, they can correct wayward commas or misspellings without needing to verify the writer's intent. But if they have questions on something more major—for example, whether a point is adequately supported or clearly expressed—then they need to speak with the writer directly and ask for clarification. Consultants can't efficiently or sustainably take the writing off colleagues' plates, but they can take responsibility for the proofreading without issue.

It's true that an abundance of grammatical errors can "slow the reader down" (May, Thompson, & Hebblethwaite, 2012, p. 262) or impact "the way the reader responds to the writer's character and intelligence" (Brandenburg, 2015, p. 84). For these reasons, writers should be encouraged to check the spelling and formatting of names, dates, and data in their writing. Some errors could damage credibility or good will with certain readers (e.g., listing a director's birth year as 1837 instead of 1937, or misgendering an individual with an innocent typo), but this has less to do with a writer's grasp on grammatical rules and more to do with proofreading habits. In one study of emails written by native and nonnative English speakers, businesspeople were less concerned with surface-level errors and were more concerned with "demanding language, casual tone, and lack of appreciation and context", as well as a lack of focus (Wolfe, Shanmugaraj, & Sipe, 2016, p. 404). At the end of the day, having other elements of writing under control should be a much higher priority than a grammatically perfect piece of writing.

Existing Guidance and Processes

Once you know where your writing center will be located (or focused) within the workplace, it's important to begin mapping out the guidance, resources, and processes that already exist for the writers you will work with. And though I've provided an overview of what writing issues you should anticipate in your workplace, you will need to explore how these appear within and are shaped by your unique environment.

Writing Guidance

Though managers and reviewers have expectations for the writing they see, they don't necessarily provide concrete guidance to writers. I've spoken with many workplace writers about how frustrating it can be to learn managers' individual preferences and to constantly modify their writing style. In other cases, writers receive feedback from their managers, but they don't understand the root cause behind changes and suggestions.

Ask people at different levels about the writing resources they use and recommend. Is there a preferred guide that writers are asked to follow (e.g., APA, CMS)? Are there standards set in place by a governing body? Is there an internal document that a group has developed to demonstrate best practices? If managers mention a preferred resource, do staff list it as one that they actually use?

If there are standards and guidance in place, be sure that your writing center adheres to them for the sake of consistent messaging and style. I have typically seen employees point to a hodgepodge of writing resources—a stapled-together packet from a workshop years ago, a guide purchased for a college course, a document saved as a model. Frequently, the resources in use contradict each other. At times, they are too focused on stylistic and editorial standards, and not focused enough on how to craft an effective message in the particular workplace context.

I recommend creating a coherent, easy-to-use writing guide as one of the first steps to promoting a workplace writing center. Chapters 5 and 6 will touch more specifically on how to create an appealing writing guide and how to use it to promote your writing center.

Manager and Staff Perspectives

The simplest way to ensure your workplace listens to the writing center is to listen to them first! Some of the most valuable insight I've gained in the beginning stages of starting a writing center has come from interviewing managers and staff separately. Invite colleagues from different levels to volunteer a half-hour block on their calendar for an interview. Make these conversations as convenient as possible: be mindful of their availability and find a convenient location (whether that means walking over to their office, booking a private conference room, or sending a link for a virtual meeting). Keep questions open-ended and consider asking some of the following.

Managers

- What writing resources have you shared with your team?
- What are some writing challenges facing your team? (Succinctness? Tone? Clarity? Applying specific conventions/language?)
- What pet peeves do you have about the writing you see?

- How do you respond if a written piece is turned in below the standard you expect? (Do you rewrite the piece directly? Pass it off to a different writer? Return it to the original writer for correction?)
- What does your team do well?
- When you provide feedback on your team's writing, do you focus on content or on features of the actual writing? How do you provide this feedback? (Verbally? Track Changes? Not at all, due to time constraints?)

Staff/Writers

- If you have a question about your writing, what resources or people do you turn to?
- What does feedback from your manager look like, and does it help you to improve?
- Do you feel that expectations for writing are clear in your team/ department? Are they consistent?
- What is the most challenging part of the writing you do on the job?
- What makes you confident about your writing?
- What resources or conversations would you find helpful as we work to make writing a less stressful process in our workplace?

Some of these questions could also be distributed by survey, but some respondents may feel uncomfortable leaving critical feedback in writing. They also may not take the time to provide a thorough answer to an open-ended question. But by having these conversations and/or collecting these data in writing, you can start to see some gaps between writers' experience and managers' expectations.

Strong and Weak Examples of Documents

Early on, begin building an arsenal of writing examples. Identify the people who are responsible for signing off on written documents (e.g., reports, memos) and ask them for copies of memorable examples. This may look like asking managers to share a "good" report and a "bad" report, taking care to specify that writers' identities should be redacted or obscured. As people submit these documents to you, ask what they consider to be "good" or "bad" features on display.

The benefits of this process are twofold. First, having real documents on hand can help you to extract relevant examples for writing guidance and workshops. And second, you may find that the documents you collect corroborate or contradict the feedback you've collected from managers and staff during your interviews. If the features of the examples corroborate any complaints you have heard from managers or any confusion you have heard from writers, then you can begin to identify areas of focus. These examples can help you to better understand the gap between what writers are working on and what managers prefer to see. In my experience, though, you are just as likely to see that department authorities aren't using or don't have the proper language to express their frustrations. For example, I have heard many managers adamantly eschew passive voice…only to find that they are actually not talking about passive voice at all, but tone, word choice, or general directness in writing. In one instance, I decided to look at the "good" example reports I had collected to see if these "good" writers had successfully avoided passive voice—they hadn't! In fact, close to 20% of the sentences in the examples were in passive voice. When I isolated these passive sentences, I found that the "good" writers were making some specific, rhetorical moves. Passive voice was used deliberately to help the audience save face or to direct the audience's attention to a particular component of a problem. Armed with these examples, I was able to clarify the messaging around passive voice that had circulated through the department for years. I explained passive voice as a tool to be used sparingly, as well as how to detect and transform it.

You may also ask writers to share documents that they reference as an example. Many writers, especially those who are novice or who lack confidence, will use prior work or someone else's work as a sort of template. This can perpetuate problems over time, since writers are returning to the same example again and again. You can also compare writers' preferred examples to those provided by management; where they align and where they differ can speak volumes.

It can also be helpful to ask managers for two drafts of the same writing sample—one that was in need of revision, and one that has since been revised and approved. This may help you understand moves made during revision processes, as well as how "bad" writing is typically transformed into "good" writing.

Report/Document Review Processes

Another crucial step is to map out review processes that exist within the workplace. Any given workplace may use a variety of formal and informal review processes, but these processes can reveal a lot about attitudes and behaviors related to revision.

Once you've identified the key written products in your workplace, ask how the process of feedback, revision, and/or approval work. Create a flowchart that explains who has a hand in revision, in what order, and with what level of authority. Ask a seasoned coworker if the process has gone through significant changes over time—and if so, what the impact was.

Many frustrations can arise from the revision. I have seen unidirectional processes where writers turn in a product, only to have it rewritten by a manager, then rewritten by a content expert, then corrected by an editor. I have seen cyclical processes where writers turn in a product and later have something unrecognizable returned to them, with no clear explanation of how to proceed. Consider posing the following questions to the writers and reviewers in your workplace as you work on your flowchart. Questions in parentheticals are options to probe for more detail or to clarify the initial question.

- Do reviewers make direct edits to written products, or do they leave comments and/or have conversations?
- What are reviewers supposed to look for? (Conceptual inconsistencies? Correctness of numbers and figures?) Do different reviewers focus on different things?
- Are the reviewers currently able to focus on what they are supposed to be focused on? (For example, are managers rewriting grammatically troubling sentences when they should be focused on subject matter/content?)
- As a document moves through the review process, do reviewers leave a trail showing who changed what? (e.g., Track Changes)
- Who has the authority to make direct changes? Is a particular reviewer(s) tasked with formal approval of the document?
- Does the original writer (or team of writers) see the final product? Do they see a record of the changes made?
- If writers are provided with a record of changes, do they take the time to look at them? Do they understand them? (This question often elicits different answers from writers and managers, which can help to identify additional disconnect).
- What happens in the review process if a reviewer determines the product is unacceptable? (Does the writer start from scratch? Is there a meeting between reviewers and the writer? Is a reviewer tasked with rewriting it?)
- Where do you see the writing center fitting in to this process? What would you find helpful?

This last question will provide insight into how people understand the writing center will work. The relationship between writing centers and formal review processes will be discussed further in the following chapter.

Manager–Staff Relationships and Performance Review Processes

A writing center in any setting should be a space where writers feel safe and comfortable sharing their writing with others. In an academic writing center, students may seek support after being referred by their professors, but professors don't typically track which of their students use the writing center. And student–professor relationships typically exist on a course-by-course basis. This is where we arrive at a major difference between academic and workplace writing centers.

In a workplace writing center, writers may be uneasy about their managers' relationship to the consultation process. I have encountered managers who have wanted to mandate the use of the writing center—some even expected that the writing center would report back on the content of these sessions and the writer's performance. Writers, naturally, become fearful that if they use the writing center, they may be perceived as remedial. Writers may also worry that if the writing center is reporting back to managers, they will be judged for any mistakes that they make in consultations. This dynamic is wildly unproductive for all involved.

Be sure to learn more about the relationship between managers and staff in your workplace, as well as whether or not writing is a component considered in performance review processes. It should be stressed early and often that writing centers do not exist to evaluate or judge the community of writers. Writing center consultations are a unique and impactful resource because they allow two experts of different backgrounds to collaborate openly and honestly, ultimately improving the writer's skills over time. If writers cannot trust what they say in sessions to stay confidential, they are unlikely to admit that they would like help or that they do not understand something. Furthermore, managers who do not have formal writing expertise may miscalculate or "misdiagnose" the challenges facing writers on their teams—this can be particularly treacherous for multilingual writers.

Negotiate ground rules with workplace leadership to ensure that the writing center can operate in a way that will build trust with writers rather than surveilling them. Consider pitching the following guidelines, but adapt them as you see fit for your workplace.

- Writing center consultations will remain as confidential as possible. What happens in a session will not be reported back to a manager. (Potential exceptions: Some writers like for their managers to know that they are putting additional effort into their writing, and they ask us to substantiate their visit. And some writers have misrepresented what was discussed in a writing center session, in which case we will share very basic notes on what was actually covered).
- The writing center will not have a formal role in the performance review process. Though managers can set writing improvement as a goal for writers on their team, the writing center will not be held accountable for specified progress.
- The writing center will not be tasked with scoring or evaluating writers, nor will consultants be responsible for enforcing use of the writing center. (Potential exceptions: The writing center may evaluate writing samples to help with hiring processes and/or to track progress within the department—more on that later).

Relationships between managers and staff tend to be longer-lasting and higher-stakes than the relationships between professors and students. Workplace writing centers must be especially careful to maintain a safe space where writers can bring all of their concerns, whether that means asking a question without shame or simply venting about frustrations within their unit.

Managers should be responsible for setting team expectations and evaluating performance, while writing centers should be responsible for supporting writers in reaching their communication-related goals.

Other Existing Services

If you are building a workplace writing center in a larger organization, it's very possible that there are already some existing writing support services in place. Take the time to learn who these people are, how they understand their work, and how those in your department understand their work. There may be a public affairs team that is responsible for maintaining standards for documents that reach the public. There may be an internal communications team that offers copyediting for messaging within the workplace. Editors may be employed to assist in research departments, or with special projects and publications.

Find out if the writers you will be working with have access to these services and/or if they are aware of them. Even more importantly, build relationships with the people who work within these other writing-related areas.

Clarifying Intent

In the past, when I was in the early stages of pitching workplace writing centers, I assumed that any editors in other departments would be thrilled to hear about writing center services. I knew that if writers came to me for help improving their writing skills, the writing that they later turned in to editors and proofreaders would be of higher quality, thus saving everyone time. This was not the case—instead, I met editors who were suspicious of my intentions. They felt that I was looking to compete with their resources and to challenge their authority on the organization's writing style. Though I had been very focused on creating a safe space for writing improvement, I had introduced a perceived threat to some of my writing colleagues.

Once you identify other writing professionals in your workplace, try to set up a casual meeting to learn more about the work that they do. Ask them about the missions set by their teams, and how they work to meet these goals. Be clear about what a writing center is, and how writing centers are vocal about not offering editing services; at the same time, express that you see their work as equally valuable, just with a different focus and set of goals. Create relationships that are complementary rather than competitive. And be sure to ask about any resources and guidance that these areas have already developed; reassure them that you are not looking to contradict what is already in place.

Establishing Collaborative Opportunities

If you build relationships with other writing professionals early on, you can find yourself with valuable allies. You can leverage each other's resources and seek each other's input. For example, when I was once developing a comprehensive writing guide for one department, I was able to seek other departments' help. A graphics department assisted with designing and printing the physical copies, an editorial department helped me to align standards with their existing guidance, and an internal communications team helped me to host this resource on an internal site. In exchange, the writing center lightened some of their workload by strengthening writers' skills, which ultimately created less revision work later on for these teams.

Summary

Though a traditional writing center model can be adapted to any type of workplace, its success will depend on how well you learn your workplace and build relationships within it. Plan ahead, but be comfortable with starting small. A well-targeted pilot can build trust and demonstrate success; a phased approach can also allow you and and/or your team time to anticipate and meet demand. Distributing surveys and identifying writing center advocates are two ways that you can narrow down an appropriate area for your pilot.

Leverage any existing guidance and standards within your workplace that you can. Not only will this prevent you from duplicating efforts, but it will also ensure consistent messaging for your colleagues. Ask about writing resources that are already in use, and begin collecting examples of "strong" and "weak" writing to inform your understanding of common writing issues and acceptable writing standards. Set up interviews with managers and with writers that are as comfortable and convenient as possible: Ask members of each group about the challenges they face and how the writing center can best support them.

Learn about the processes and relationships that are well established in your workplace. Build trust with other writing professionals in your workplace, explaining the purpose of the writing center and how it can complement the work that they do. Within your own work, create a flowchart of review processes so that you can better understand frustrations arising from various points of revision. Set clear expectations and boundaries with workplace leadership regarding the writing center's role. Managers and supervisors should be responsible for performance reviews and evaluations, while the writing center should serve as a safe, neutral space of support. If writers see the writing center as a professional development resource that will allow them as much confidentiality as possible, your writing center will be on a path to success.

Note

1 The "sandwich method" is the practice of burying an unsavory point in between two more positive ones, in order to make it more palatable. For instance: *We've loved having you at this company. Unfortunately, your position has been eliminated. But we'll let you take this mug with you!*

References

Bernoff, J. (2016). *Writing without bullshit: Boost your career by saying what you mean.* New York: HarperBusiness.

Brandenburg, L. C. (2015). Testing the recognition and perception of errors in context. *Business and Professional Communication Quarterly, 78*(1), 74–93. https://doi.org/10.1177/2329490614563570

French, S. L., & Holden, T. Q. (2012). Positive organizational behavior: A buffer for bad news. *Business Communication Quarterly, 75*(2), 208–220. https://doi.org/10.1177/1080569912441823

Friess, E. (2013). "Bring the newbie into the fold": Politeness strategies of newcomers and existing group members within workplace meetings. *Technical Communication Quarterly, 22*(4), 304–322. https://doi-org.lib-e2.lib.ttu.edu/10.1080/10572252.2013.782261

Greer, R. R. (2012). Introducing plain language principles to business communication students. *Business Communication Quarterly, 75*(2), 136–152. https://doi.org/10.1177/1080569912441967

Jameson, D. A. (2009). Management consulting and teaching: Lessons learned teaching professionals to control tone in writing. *Business and Professional Communication Quarterly, 72*(3), 333–338.

Jones, N., McDavid, J., Derthick, K., Dowell, R., & Spyridakis, J. (2012). Plain language in environmental policy documents: An assessment of reader comprehension and perceptions. *Journal of Technical Writing and Communication, 42*(4), 77–97.

Mabrito, M. (1997). Writing on the front line: A study of workplace writing. *Business Communication Quarterly, 60*(3), 58–70.

May, G. L., Thompson, M. A., & Hebblethwaite, J. (2012). A process for assessing and improving business writing at the MBA level. *Business Communication Quarterly, 75*(3), 252–270. https://doi.org/10.1177/1080569912441822

Walton, R. (2013). How trust and credibility affect technology-based development projects. *Technical Communication Quarterly, 22*(1), 85–102. https://doi-org.libe2.lib.ttu.edu/10.1080/10572252.2013.726484

Weber, R. (2013). Constrained agency in corporate social media policy. *Journal of Technical Writing & Communication, 43*(3), 289–315. https://doi-org.lib-e2.lib.ttu.edu/10.2190/TW.43.3.d

Wolfe, J., Shanmugaraj, N., & Sipe, J. (2016). Grammatical versus pragmatic error: Employer perceptions of nonnative and native English speakers. *Business and Professional Communication Quarterly, 79*(4), 397–415. https://doi.org/10.1177/2329490616671133

5 Determining Services

Once you have learned more about the relationships, processes, and existing guidance within your workplace, it's time to determine what services will best serve writers. This chapter will cover some core services that I have implemented within workplaces, including one-on-one consultations, creating writing guidance, and delivering custom workshops.

The Space of the Writing Center

Before we dive into core services, let's take a moment to consider the space—both physical and virtual—that your writing center will occupy. Any time that I have pitched a workplace writing center, I have been adamant about reserving a physical space within the workplace. Sometimes this has looked like a small office just big enough for a desk, a table, and two chairs; sometimes this has looked like a state-of-the-art conference room with couches and tables and an abundance of natural light. As long as the space is visible, inviting, and allows for some privacy, it should work just fine.

Physical Space

Ideally, situate your writing center close to the primary group of writers it will serve, or at least somewhere with a decent amount of foot traffic. Place a sign—no matter how fancy or handmade—near or on the writing center door so that it is clearly marked. I have done this even in cases where the writing center doubles as my private office. Depending on the building's layout, you may want to introduce yourself to people stationed by entrances to your floor or department. I've found that many of these people end up serving as impromptu guides for those who enter their area looking lost.

Consider ways in which you can make the writing center space inviting. Perhaps you will have the budget to set up a coffee machine or other amenities (if so, I am envious…but I have also found that a bowl of candy or a box of tea will also do the trick). Whenever possible, keep the lights on and the doors open. Even when a writing center has doubled as a private office for me, I have marketed it as a shared space where anyone is welcome to come and work quietly. Occasionally, writers take me up on this offer, sharing that they can

DOI: 10.4324/9781003212959-8

concentrate better in a different space, and that it is helpful to ask me occasional questions as they write. This space can also be helpful if writers are in and out of the office for travel and offsite work; sometimes the writers I work with do not have a designated desk at all.

As your writing center becomes more established, curate a collection of resources and consider allowing brief loans. In one of my first weeks at my first workplace writing center, I would load up a suitcase with my writing guides and textbooks every morning and drag it on to the 57 bus. It took three or four days to bring in all of my resources, and I'm fairly certain that the security guards at work thought I was moving in. I later found out that my department had a designated budget for educational resources, and I was then able to order copies of books that my colleagues would find helpful while they were writing. Over time, I managed to cobble together a bookshelf full of business writing guides, citation style guides, and textbooks. I invite my colleagues to look through the bookshelves, and to take notes and photocopies as they need. I also bring many of these resources into consultations as a way to bring in additional viewpoints and examples.

Privacy is an important element of a writing center. In a busy academic writing center, this may mean spacing out tables as best one can, or designating a more private area tucked in near a bookshelf. In a workplace writing center, the option to close a door is best. Writing is an inherently personal thing, even if the subject matter is not particularly personal. I have helped writers work through frustration, lack of confidence, and anxiety as they write and revise—I am not a therapist, of course, but I can provide them with a peaceful space where they can feel comfortable asking questions and sharing their thoughts. When a student comes to an academic writing center, they are unlikely to run in to their professor while working on an assignment; when a writer comes to a workplace writing center, however, their manager may be seated just a few offices away. This privacy is especially important when working within one-on-one consultations.

Virtual Space

I write this during an extended period of telework during the Covid-19 pandemic, and it has been over a year since I have been able to step into the physical space of our writing center. At no point before have so many offices been engaged in conversations about what it will look like to bring staff back into buildings or whether they will allow telework arrangements: This is just one of many reasons to consider the virtual space of your writing center.

An important first step is to learn what software and resources are available to you and your colleagues. Can you host virtual one-on-one meetings over a particular video chat platform? Do you have access to software that can be helpful when leading virtual workshops (e.g., virtual classroom spaces and/or polling software for audience engagement)? Do writers consistently engage with or have a basic familiarity with this software, or has there been resistance?

Do the writers you'll work with have access to a phone and/or audio-only web calls as well?

Additionally, consider where you can host information about and resources from your writing center. A simple webpage hosted on your intranet could allow writers to book consultations, read about services, view instructional modules, and access digital copies of writing guidance and handouts. I have even seen some of these sites feature a rotating consultant who is available for questions via chat. Updates, news articles, and even a regular newsletter can also be shared through this online hub. The next chapter will cover more about creating a website while developing your branding and marketing strategies.

But even before the near-overnight shift to remote work, I found that almost half of the writers I work with regularly use virtual rather than in-person services. These writers were already working from home part-time, or traveling to conferences, or completing their duties at other designated worksites. Allowing these writers to call or video chat consultants for support, as well as access our resources from afar, helps keep them connected and supported as they write. Overall, the more varied and creative ways that we are able to reach writers, the more ways we will create meaningful connections with them.

One-on-One Consultations

One-on-one writing consultations are a writing center's signature service, allowing writers flexibility and individualized instruction. Though workshops and other modes of support are common in writing centers as well, "[a]dult learners attend best to what they actually need on any given day" (Warner & Hewett, 2017). Individual consultations allow for writers to ask questions unique to their situations, to focus on their most pressing concerns, and to practice skills related to their current assignments. In one study, the indicators for a positive learning experience—"self-efficacy, learning goal orientation, and motivation to learn"—were all tied to the participant's active engagement and "willingness to learn for self-development" (Charoensap-Kelly, Broussard, Lindsly, & Troy, 2016, p. 159). This engagement and openness are both prerequisites to scheduling a one-on-one writing consultation, so each session should serve as a positive learning experience for the writer.

Offering one-on-one consultations also allows writers to work around their individual schedules. One major difference between learning in educational settings and in workplace settings is that in workplace settings, people usually must come and go as their work schedules allow. This can include last-minute assignments or crises that pop up and pull the writer away from a scheduled workshop or class. Such distractions and sudden schedule changes can be disruptive not only for the writer, but for the other workshop participants as well (Gygi & Zachry, 2010, p. 376). One-on-one sessions allow workshop participants (or those who could not attend the workshops) the opportunity to fill in any gaps in their learning.

Though you will want to consider your workplace's unique writers and written products, here are a number of best practices that I have found success with in a variety of settings.

Before the Consultation

Ask writers to request consultations in advance. Though allowing some walk-in consultations can help writers with less predictable schedules, having advance-notice policies can make things run more smoothly for everyone involved. At least 24 hours' notice when booking a consultation is a good benchmark, and writers should be encouraged to submit the piece they are working on in advance. In your booking processes, you may also consider asking writers to select areas of focus for their session (e.g., organization, tone). This advance notice allows the designated consultant to review the piece, identify patterns of error or themes, and gather notes and resources before the one-on-one session.

Having clear procedures and boundaries related to consultations helps protect the time of both the writers and the writing center team. Writers can be assured that if they book consultations in advance, they will experience a focused, individualized, and well-thought-out consultation when they show up (or call in). And writing center teams can have their time protected and their work valued. All too often, people underestimate the amount of time and effort that goes into consultants preparing for sessions. It's not uncommon to see a writer submit a 50-page report when requesting a session for that same afternoon. In these cases, I encourage writing center consultants to gently remind writers of the advance notice policy and to ask the writer to schedule several sessions to get through a document of that size. Though it may take some time for writers to understand and respect these policies, ultimately the policies are meant to keep both parties from becoming fatigued and frustrated.

Booking procedures need not be complicated. Though you can use scheduling software or build an online form, you can just as easily begin with a simple email template. Here is an example with some recommended fields.

You can modify this form in any way that makes sense for your writing center. If several types of documents or written projects are common in your workplace, you may consider modifying the "Please describe what you are working on" field with multiple-choice (and "other") options. You can also include any policy reminders about advance notice requirements and/or what time zone your writing center operates in (if your workforce is more dispersed).

During the Consultation

If a writer has correctly filled out the session request form, then the consultant will know whether this is the writer's first use of the service. When consultants are working with new writers, they let the writer know what to expect in the session. Writers are reminded that their sessions will be kept as confidential as

Name: _____

Requested Consultation Date: _____

Requested Consultation Time (30- or 60-minute block): _____

Is this your first time using the Writing Center?

❏ Yes ❏ No

Please describe what you are working on: _____

What is the deadline for this project? _____

What would you like to focus on in your consultation?

❏ Organization ❏ Tone

❏ Support/Analysis ❏ Grammar/Proofreading

❏ Clarity ❏ Citations

❏ Bottom Line Up Front ❏ ESL/Multilingual Writing

❏ Other: _____

How would you like to meet with your consultant?

❏ In Person

❏ Video Chat

❏ Phone Call

Please upload or attach a copy of the project you are working on, unless this will be a brainstorming/work-in-progress session.

possible, and that the goal is to improve their writing skills rather than to produce a perfect, error-free document. If a writer has been to the writing center several times before, then consultants can look back at session log notes from previous sessions. Reading through log notes can help consultants to scaffold on the conversations and lessons shared in past sessions.

Writing consultants should employ the same indirect tutoring methods that would be used in an academic writing center. They should ask questions that lead writers to greater understanding of their writing, rather than giving direct advice. Consultant feedback should be contextualized as reader response from a different perspective, and the writer's expertise should be acknowledged. All too often, I have watched as writers eagerly wrote down my suggestions word-for-word, assuming I was giving them the "correct" answers. Instead, I want them to realize that they have the ultimate authority over how their message will best reach their readers, and that I (or another consultant) is there to help them think through the tools and strategies at their disposal.

Consultants should try to be hands-off when they are looking at a writer's document. Though they make notes on their own copy while preparing for a session, they should not send direct revisions to the writer. If a writer sees corrections in a document, they are likely to accept changes without thinking critically about them or learning anything valuable from the experience. In an in-person session, consultants can hand a pen or pencil to the writer for any notes, and put their own hands in their lap; they can also share a copy between them but make clear that the writer will be the only one taking notes, and only on what suggestions the writer chooses to apply. In a remote session, consultants should make use of screen-sharing technology when possible. It can help for writer and consultant to look at the same spaces in a document; however, the consultant should take care not to show a marked-up version, which is likely to lead to the writer's reliance on copying down corrections.

After the Consultation

Once the consultation ends, the consultant should log session notes in a central database (more on this in Chapter 8). Notes should be respectful but specific, capturing what was discussed in the session and whether the writer seemed engaged and open to suggestions. You may also consider having consultants send a follow-up email after the session with some very general notes on what was discussed in the session. It can be helpful for writers to have this additional touchpoint, as well as for consultants to have a record of what was communicated in the session.

A follow-up email is also a good opportunity for consultants to link to additional resources that may be helpful as the writer makes their revisions. This follow-up email may also contain a link to a feedback survey for the writer to fill out (more on feedback surveys in Chapter 9).

Be mindful of any document handling guidance that your workplace has in place. You may find yourself working with writers on sensitive or confidential documents; ensure you are managing and disposing of files (print and digital) according to your organization's standards.

Creating a Standard Writing Guide

Chapter 4 detailed a number of examples and resources to procure in order to better learn your workplace's unique writing style. By interviewing managers and staff, you can learn about the most pressing concerns and areas of focus related to writing. And by collecting examples of different work products (both "good" and "bad" versions) you will be able to demonstrate writing strategies within recognizable contexts. Following are some best practices for creating a writing guide that your writers will actually want to use.

Appearance

The ideal writing guide is approachable and easy to use. In my own days as an academic tutor, the guide I reached for most was Diana Hacker and Nancy Sommers' *A Pocket Style Manual*. It was lightweight, color-coded, and spiral-bound—easy to flip through and find exactly the information I was looking for. I replicated many of these features the first time that I created an in-house writing style guide. Because the resulting product was so easy to tuck away in a laptop bag or a desk drawer, both on-site and off-site writers were happy to keep a copy with them. The information within was comprehensive, totaling close to a 100 pages, but the book itself was small and lightweight enough to be unintimidating.

Though having physical copies of writing guidance is helpful for more tactile learners and even for marketing purposes, it is equally important to offer a digital version. Hosting a version of the guide online and/or creating a PDF version will help it to reach even more people. Digital guides can be more easily shared and accessed, especially while writers work from the road or from home. You may even include instructions in the physical copy of the guide on how to access a digital version.

Explore whether you can leverage any in-house or local design and print services. Larger workplaces may have graphic designers on staff who are able to lend a hand as you determine layout and design. Your workplace may have a designated printer that you will need to go through, or you may be able to produce copies from within your workplace. Approach any potential collaborators early in the process to be sure you're following all policies and guidelines. Determine what budget you may have to work with, and look into potential publishing costs. Keep in mind that the length of your guide, the number of copies you will need, and the amount of color you include can all change related prices. It may be helpful to know this information before you begin polishing drafts of your guide.

Organization and Suggested Content

Workplace writers are often more concerned about producing a grammatically correct/error-free piece than about making sure their message is rhetorically sound—in other words, they tend to focus on lower-order concerns rather than on higher-order concerns. For this reason, I would recommend structuring your writing guide so that higher-order concerns are toward the beginning. Writers are likely to assume that guidance will mostly cover surface-level issues like punctuation and commonly confused words; beginning with bigger concepts like organization, tone, and clarity can help reset their focus. You might even include a description in the beginning of the guide that explains how to use it or where users should spend the most time. As a starting point, you can consider the writing components outlined in Chapter 4. Most recently, I designed a guide that opened with general rhetorical elements of writing, then organizational techniques, then sentence structure (including supporting and analysis), then word choice (including clarity and tone), then finally grammar, mechanics, and stylistic features.

Helpful Features

Choose a font and size that will be easily legible both on the page and on a screen. Use colors to help organize information and to make certain features stand out; however, ensure that your use of color does not present any difficulties for readers with colorblindness or visual impairments. Generally, minimize the length of paragraphs used in your guide. Instead of dense paragraphs, consider using bullet points, boxes, and graphic organizers to present information in a visually pleasing and efficient way. As an example, I have designed guides that have used blue boxes to highlight summary information and main ideas, and yellow boxes to highlight tips and tricks.

Writers have shared with me that one of their favorite aspects of the guides are the "tips and tricks" boxes that we've included. Some of these tricks are specifically relevant to writing, like explaining reverse outlining techniques or sharing proofreading suggestions. Others are more related to writing in a digital environment, like keyboard shortcuts and how to use text-to-speech or read-aloud functions.

Another popular feature has been our use of relevant examples throughout the guide. Each section includes an example that we've modified from a real work product, so the language and situation look familiar to writers. I've commonly followed a predictable structure in the guides I've worked on: first, an introduction of a particular writing concept; second, an example of the concept being ignored or incorrectly applied, highlighted in a red box; and third, an example of a [revised] sentence that does follow the advice given, highlighted in a green box. These boxes also use recurring symbols (e.g., a red "X" and a green check mark) to aid those who can distinguish colors less easily. This structure not only helps writers to understand the concepts you're explaining, but it allows them a chance to practice revising if they only look at the red, incorrect boxes and then check their work in the green, correct boxes.

Involve Your Workplace Writers and Leaders

Pay attention to respected voices in your workplace. Though you may be trusted with providing writing guidance and advice, there are always some seasoned colleagues whose voices hold particular weight. Some of the writing guides I've created have opened with the "top ten pieces of advice from managers and executive leaders", a feature which has gotten writers' attention and buy-in. These particular pieces of advice came from interviews with managers that I conducted in my early days of establishing a writing center. Before you begin (or complete) your writing guide, you should also reach out to writers to learn what it is that they want to see covered.

Equally important is providing a channel for feedback. Perhaps you can enlist a few writers to provide feedback on a draft before you publish copies for your workplace. Or, you can include information in the guide about how to get in touch with questions and suggestions. It's important to see writing guidance as a living document; the nature of your workplace's work and writing are likely to shift over time, and so should the guidance you share. Be prepared to create new editions of the guide every few years or as necessary. The feedback that you collect from writers between editions will be helpful as you make changes and improvements.

Custom Workshops

In the workplace, writing workshops are perhaps the most recognizable writing center service. But traditionally, workplaces hire an outside writing expert or company to lead a limited series of generic workshops. Workshops offered by an embedded workplace writing center can offer a variety of benefits at a fraction of the cost. Not only can writing centers offer workshops on a continuous basis, allowing for refresher courses and for ongoing training of new employees, but they can also make instruction specific to the writers' everyday tasks. Furthermore, the relationship that your writing consultants will build with writers by virtue of being in the same environment every day is invaluable. Every effort should be taken to build trust between writers and consultants, creating a respectful, peer-to-peer rapport that is preserved even in workshop settings.

Of all writing center services, workshops are also the closest to resemble traditional classroom instruction. But with the right measures, you can keep learning collaborative rather than seen as information passively passed from expert to learner. Organize writers into clusters of desks or break-out groups whenever possible, allowing for easier facilitation of peer-to-peer group activities (Gygi & Zachry, 2010). Peer groups can be arranged with physical tables in a conference room or even through virtual break-out rooms online. Workshop leaders should seek to keep workshops engaging. Allow for breaks to practice the skills being discussed, to talk about current projects in small groups, and to apply new lessons to a piece of writing that is currently on their to-do list already.

It's additionally important to ensure that employees move away from the common assumption that workplace writing is primarily prescriptive or template-driven. Yes, writers frequently work with common forms, genres, and even physical templates, but they need to do much more than simply plug in the correct information. These workshops or other learning opportunities may address the ways in which employees use resources, as well as best practices (Gygi & Zachry, 2010).

It's important to communicate, both before and during any workshop offerings, that the workshop is efficient for its focus "on communication strategies rather than on more narrowly defined standards for correct writing" (Gygi & Zachry, 2010, p. 374). Writers are likely to walk in to (or sign on to) workshops with the expectation that they will be doing grammar drills. But if you've established a writing guide or standards in your workplace, you can point writers there for the "rules", encouraging them to think about workshops instead as more conversational, focused on big-picture strategy and hands-on practice. Workshops are also a good opportunity to remind writers of one-on-one consultation services available, which will further supplement and individualize their learning.

Though writing centers are still a brand-new concept for many nonacademic spaces, we do know how workplace training tends to compare to classroom training. One study showed that workplace learning is *"more clearly defined, more collaborative,* and *more innovative,* but also that it is *less supportive* and is *characterized by less independence"* (Smith, 2003, p. 67, emphasis author's). The second part of this conclusion is troubling: that workplace learners feel less supported and less independent. Any workplace writing center should take care to avoid these dynamics. This may involve investigating if employees feel micromanaged (in which case, excluding managers/supervisors from workshop attendance may be helpful), or if feeling as though a one-time workshop did not provide enough guidance. Those who attend writing workshops or use one-on-one consultations are only likely to remember a few pieces of advice; but what they will absolutely remember is how they felt in that space. Creating a safe environment, communicating expectations clearly, and providing ongoing, individualized support can help to establish a successful center.

Remote Services

In my experience, writers have responded much more positively to in-person workshops than to workshops hosted online. But remote instruction is an important consideration for a more dispersed and/or flexible workplace, especially if opportunities for travel to a common site are limited. These resources could take the form of a synchronous workshop hosted through a video conferencing service, or a series of recorded video modules that can be watched at the viewer's pace. It's wise to take advantage of the technology available in your workplace, but it's also valuable to consider what your target audience of writers see as worthwhile.

One-on-one remote writing consultations, however, have historically been a more popular option than remote workshops in the centers I've advised. This preference is likely because participation is easier in a one-on-one remote session than it is in an online classroom setting. About half of the writing consultations I've led in different workplaces have been remote, conducted over video or phone; it's an especially appealing option for writers who telework or travel for work. In the past 10 or 15 years, the academic writing center community has also seen an uptick in online services and remote offerings. But in a survey published in 2009, Neaderhiser and Wolfe found that "99% of reported online consultations conducted in 2005–2006 used text-based technologies", with very few institutions taking advantage of synchronous tools like web conferencing or even phone calls (p. 69). The study concludes with a call for more research into online consultations; this call is one that may be answered, in part, by workplaces willing to explore writing centers and remote consultations. By 2014–2015, the Writing Centers Research Project reported that "59% of respondents offered online or virtual services", up from "53% offering online services in 2006" (Prince, Willard, Zamarripa, & Sharkey-Smith, 2018, p. 12).

All of the writing centers that I have worked in firsthand generally cautioned against conducting writing center sessions over email or text-based mediums. Providing in-text revisions for the writer allows them to simply copy-paste or accept-all changes to their work, without really learning the reason for the change or how to apply it in the future. In general, there has been a lack of literature related to online tutoring. Most research has focused instead on online teaching; this research cannot necessarily be directly applied to online tutoring. As Muriel Harris explicitly states on IWCA's website, the relationship between tutor and tutee and teacher and student are not equivalent (Prince et al., 2018, p. 14). Tutoring relationships are meant to be more individualized and collaborative.

But those who *have* researched and written about online tutoring and consulting relationships have had positive things to say. Not only do some writing center professionals say that relationships they build with those accessing services remotely do not differ significantly from those who visit the writing center in person, but they even point out some advantages (Summers, 2012, p. 11). One such advantage is that physical distance allows writers to "slip into a more natural writing mode without feeling like the consultant is left waiting" because a Skype window is easier to ignore than a consultant sitting at the same table (Summers, 2012, p. 12). In my experience, writers seem more eager to accept phone or audio-only web calls than video calls. This may be because turning off one's webcam allows for this feeling of distance and privacy. Audio-only web calls are still useful because consultants can use screen-sharing functions and be sure that they're looking at the same part of the document that the writer is. I have noticed that writers working physically side-by-side with consultants can seem rushed while taking notes or making revisions, possibly because the waiting consultant is within their immediate view, so I think this speculation holds true for my writing center experience, as well.

Overall, any workplace seeking to create their own writing center would be wise to consider offering remote options for one-on-one consultations. Online training is not only "flexible, convenient, and cost-effective" (Charoensap-Kelly et al., 2016, p. 161), but also does not differ in effectiveness as long as participants demonstrate a willingness to learn (p. 168). I've witnessed writers accessing remote consultations with the same consultant for several years. These relationships are every bit as real as those forged in person—complete with learning, questions, and occasional laughter. One disadvantage that is occasionally pointed out by the literature in online training is that participants have a limited capacity to "ask questions, provide feedback, interact with peers, and practice the skills in a natural setting" (Charoensap-Kelly et al., 2016, p. 161). However, each of these concerns is eliminated or at least greatly reduced in remote consultations (as opposed to remote group training). Remote consultations, just like in-person consultations, should be designed to be conversational: Writers ask questions, consultants deliver specific feedback, and both parties take the time that they need to apply skills and check for effective revision strategies.

Text-Based Revision Services

As I've made clear throughout this chapter, the more that writers take control of their own revisions and skill work, the more they will benefit. Editorial and proofreading services are valuable at ending stages of the writing process, but they are best offered through editorial teams (see Chapter 4, "Other Existing Services"). It will take any writing center a good period of time to successfully communicate their role in the workplace; even after several years, you are likely to hear from writers who still want to "drop off their pieces" to be "fixed". If editing and proofreading services are offered through your writing center, the messaging around and benefits of your other services are likely to be conflated or outright ignored. I recommend taking a firm stance against transactional editing services, though I always permit writers to work on grammar and proofreading within a one-on-one consultation.

However, I *have* worked with workplaces to incorporate writing consultants into formal writing review processes. In these cases, I've negotiated with reporting lines and reviewers at different levels to determine how the writing center can be helpful without compromising other writing center services. Chapter 4 advises creating a flowchart of revision processes. Writing consultants can carefully offer feedback within this process; perhaps the consultant can leave comments about higher-order issues that the writer can incorporate during revision, or can even provide a final back-end proofread. Some writers may feel more comfortable working on higher-order concerns in consultations if they know that their work will get a final edit before it's delivered to a high-stakes audience. Text-based comments in the revision process may also be another opportunity for consultants to remind writers that they can access feedback and support earlier on in the writing process. But whether you decide to have your writing center consultants participate in formal review processes or not, this is something that should be delicately navigated and then communicated to all writers, reviewers, and other writing experts involved.

Summary

There is much to consider when it comes to determining the services your writing center will offer, but you are likely to find success if you focus on meeting writers where they are. Consider what your writing center will look like in both in-person and in online spaces, and ensure that all writers will feel welcome there. Provide consistent guidance through regularly-updated writing guides or other easy-to-reference resources.

Focus on one-on-one writing consultations as your writing center's signature service. These consultations are truly what set writing centers apart from other existing writing support services (including external workshops and internal editorial services). Allow for flexibility in how writers can access and individualize these consultations, but encourage consultants to use nondirect, scaffolded instruction that builds on writers' understanding and skills.

Offering regular writing workshops is another helpful extension of writing support, as well as a way to keep center services on writers' radar. Be sure to keep workshops as engaging, writer-focused, and relevant as possible. Consider whether remote consultations are a worthwhile offering to explore, as well.

It's also important to determine whether or not your writing center will play any role in revision and/or editing services within formal review processes. No matter what you decide, be sure to keep messaging about the writing center's purpose—improved writers, not perfected documents—clear. The next chapter will help you explore the best ways to sharpen and deliver the branding and messaging around your writing center.

References

Charoensap-Kelly, P., Broussard, L., Lindsly, M., & Troy, M. (2016). Evaluation of a soft skills training program. *Business and Professional Communication Quarterly, 79*(2), 154–179. https://doi.org/10.1177/2329490615602090

Gygi, K., & Zachry, M. (2010). Productive tensions and the regulatory work of genres in the development of an engineering communication workshop in a transnational corporation. *Journal of Business and Technical Communication, 24*(3), 358–381. https://doi.org/10.1177/1050651910363365

Neaderhiser, S., & Wolfe, J. (2009). Between technological endorsement and resistance: The state of online writing centers. *Writing Center Journal, 29*(1), 49–77.

Prince, S., Willard, R., Zamarripa, E., & Sharkey-Smith, M. (2018). Peripheral (re)visions: Moving online writing centers from margin to center. *WLN: A Journal of Writing Center Scholarship, 42*(5–6), 10–16. Retrieved from https://wlnjournal.org/archives/v42/42.5-6.pdf

Smith, P. J. (2003, Spring). Workplace learning and flexible delivery. *Review of Educational Research, 73*(1). Retrieved from https://www.jstor.org/stable/3516043

Summers, S. (2012). Delivering distance consultations with Skype and Google Docs. *Writing Lab Newsletter, 37*(7–8), 10–13. Retrieved from https://wlnjournal.org/archives/v37/37.7-8.pdf

Warner, R. Z., & Hewett, B. L. (2017). Technical communication coaching: A strategy for instilling reader usability assurance in online course material development. *Technical Communication Quarterly, 26*(3), 300–313. https://doi.org/10.1080/1057225 2.2017.1339493

6 Branding and Marketing

No matter how solidly you've planned your writing center, it will only be impactful if employees are actually willing to use it. Therefore, the messaging around your writing center is extremely important. This chapter will offer guidance on crafting a mission statement, developing a brand, and marketing writing center services within your workplace.

Crafting a Mission Statement

Your writing center's mission statement will not only guide the strategic planning and day-to-day operations of the center, but should also communicate values and areas of focus. Mission statements are best kept "brief and general", but should "name commitments to quality and service and as such serve as means by which an institution or instructional site can hold itself accountable to the constituencies it serves to seek" (Condon, 2007, p. 23). Revisit your mission statement often to ensure this accountability and focus.

First and foremost, consider the writers that you will serve, as well as the workplace itself. Use language that will resonate with and appeal to these audiences. In "The (Un)Importance of a Preposition: How We Define and Defend Writing Center work", Tabetha Adkins praises the following components of a mission statement (2011, p. 3):

- Who the writing center helps
- Methods or approaches that the writing center uses
- Why these methods or approaches are used

A fourth component that Adkins admires is a clear statement about what the writing center *does not* do (e.g., editing, proofreading, "drop-off" or "fix-it" services). While this is, in fact, a common feature of many university writing center's mission statements, Muriel Harris cautions against such negative language (2010, p. 55). Harris argues that statements dispelling myths or excluding services actually draw readers' attention to those assumptions; additionally, using a negative tone can compromise your message's tone. On the other hand, "research affirms the familiar rhetorical principle: messages phrased affirmatively are more effective than messages phrased negatively" (p. 55).

DOI: 10.4324/9781003212959-9

You can find an abundance of writing center mission statements online, since most university and college writing centers have webpages. At the time of this writing, Allison Hutchison has also compiled and made available a document with 100 writing center mission statements.[1] Perusing some of these samples may be helpful as you craft your own, but keep in mind that there is no perfect ideal that you need to match. Muriel Harris points to the fact that "writing center professionals have not identified universally applicable positive frames that are powerful and memorable", which is actually a strength (2010, p. 52). A variety of mission statements and frameworks allows for "[w]riting centers in different institutions, cultures, countries, and continents" to be "structured to meet different needs" (2010, p. 52). The best mission statement is the one that most effectively relays your services and values to your intended audience and stakeholders.

When you do land on a suitable mission statement, be sure to feature it prominently. It should be easily found on your writing center's webpage, and may also be displayed within a physical writing center or on "any promotional materials the writing center distributes" (Adkins, 2011, p. 3). Use your mission statement to aid writers' understanding of available services, as well as to ensure consistency of service from multiple writing center consultants. Be sure to consult your writing center team (if assembled) as you draft your mission statement, and involve them in a review of it at least every year or so.

Logo and Branding

After consistent messaging, one of the best things you can do as you create your writing center is to build a recognizable brand. The access that you may have to marketing and design services or software is likely to vary by the size of your workplace—but even with fewer resources, you can still utilize several branding strategies.

It's worth investigating whether your workplace has a graphic design team, and if so, whether that team can help you to develop a logo. Pay attention to promotional materials that other departments or services within your workplace use, and ask how they were able to develop logos or other markers. Perhaps you can't outsource this work to an internal (or external) design team, but you may be able to purchase a copy of basic design software and tinker around. Even in a small workplace or one with fewer resources, you can still make consistent choices that make your writing center more recognizable. You can choose a simple, free-use icon online and pair it with a consistent font and color. It doesn't need to be fancy. It just needs to be recognizable over time. Not only does branding help writers and stakeholders to identify the writing center's materials and spaces, but it also helps people to perceive the writing center as a respectable, well-established resource. And for a team of consultants, it can build a sense of pride, as well.

You might consider using your logo or other branding items in or on the following spaces:

- Writing center web page
- Business cards for writing center consultants
- A sign for the physical writing center
- Presentation slides used in workshops
- Digital or print handout resources
- Background images for consultants to use during video consultations
- The cover of a writing guide

If you are able to order or access personalized promotional items, this is also a great way to draw attention to your resource. I have found writing center-branded pens to be a popular giveaway with writers who attend a consultation or workshop in person. And even with a very limited budget, you could get creative in the same way that many funding-strapped academic writing centers have: Print and distribute paper bookmarks that include information about the writing center.

Online Presence

Writers working within a communal office as well as offsite will benefit from an easy-to-navigate, resource-laden writing center website. Your writing center's webpage is likely to be housed within your workplace's intranet, but there may be exceptions. Familiarize yourself with the ways that other units or departments share their work and services internally, and reach out to IT teams or web support teams to learn how you can establish an online presence as well.

If you have control over the look and feel of the page, be sure to select a font type, size, and color that is easy to see against a simple background. Keep information organized and text brief so that readers can easily take in information and follow links to more. And of course, incorporate any branding that you may have developed for your writing center.

Consider including the following features or sections on your writing center webpage.

- **Home.** Include general information about the writing center, including its mission statement, currently offered services, hours of operation, and location. You may also want to include a testimonial or two. Alternatively, this may be a "Dashboard"-style page wherein viewers can navigate to other areas of the website.
- **Appointment Scheduling.** Ideally, you will be able to host some kind of online scheduler so that writers can seamlessly request consultations during writing center consultants' available time slots. Though there are many tutor scheduling software options to choose from, workplaces are already likely to have their own policies, procedures, or habits in place

already—in my own experience, purchasing additional scheduling software has not been a practical route. In the past, I have worked with internal business technology teams to develop a sleek scheduling system... but I have also used solutions that are much simpler. For instance, you can simply consider the scheduling software that is already in use in your workplace. How do you book an appointment with a colleague, send an invite for a team meeting, or block off a work friend's calendar for lunch? Use this existing infrastructure and ask writers to attach or submit an appointment request form (an example is shown in Chapter 5) to collect additional data. But no matter which appointment scheduling procedures you put in place, be sure to have directions clearly spelled out for writers who land on your appointment scheduling page.

- **Resources.** Create a hub for resources that can be accessed online. This may include links to video modules that your writing center has created. You can link to downloadable copies of a writing guide or digital handouts on specific concepts. You may also choose to link to other resources available within your workplace, or to external sites that writers may find helpful (e.g., the Purdue OWL, Dave's ESL Café).

- **News and Notes.** Keep writers and stakeholders in the loop with this frequently updated page. You can upload quarterly newsletters or even link to any internal or external news about what your writing center have accomplished.

- **Workshops and Events.** If you will be offering workshops on a rolling basis in your workplace, you can advertise them here and provide relevant links for sign-up. You may also include information about how people can request additional support from the writing center. For example, you may have a form for managers who wish to request a custom workshop for their team, or a form to request a writing center information booth at an upcoming internal event (e.g., some larger organizations host professional development or benefits "information fairs").

- **About.** An "about" page can help provide a clearer picture of your writing center, as well as answer lingering questions that the viewer may have. You can host your mission statement and list your services here if you haven't done so on your home page. You can also include a little bit of background about how and why the writing center was founded within your organization. You may also include information about different consultants on your team, especially if writers have the ability to request who they would like to work with (this is a common feature on academic writing center pages). It may also help to share writing center consultants' credentials and experience as a way of building additional trust in the writing center.

- **Contact.** If not listed elsewhere, it can be helpful to have a general contact form or to list a shared email inbox for the writing center. This allows for people to reach you with general questions, feedback, or other requests that you may not have thought of yet.

Ultimately, your writing center's online presence should be designed with your audience's needs and your workplace's existing parameters in mind. Solicit feedback from users as you put together your webpage, and be sure to update and check links often to ensure that they are working.

Summary

Access to branding strategies, expertise, and resources varies wildly between different workplaces. Make good use of what is available to you, and don't be afraid to get creative! What's most important is building a brand that is consistent, recognizable, and carefully aligned with the writing center's mission. With consistent language and imagery, you can earn the trust of writers and stakeholders, encouraging them to use the services you'll offer.

Note

1 https://allisonhutchison.github.io/Writing%20Center%20Mission%20Statements.pdf.

References

Adkins, T. (2011). The (un)importance of a preposition: How we define and defend writing center work. *WLN: A Journal of Writing Center Scholarship, 36*(1–2), 1–5. Retrieved from https://wlnjournal.org/archives/v36/36.1-2.pdf.

Condon, F. (2007). Beyond the known: Writing centers and the work of anti-racism. *The Writing Center Journal, 27*(2), 19–38. Retrieved April 18, 2021, from http://www.jstor.org/stable/43442270

Harris, M. (2010). Making our institutional discourse sticky: Suggestions for effective rhetoric. *The Writing Center Journal, 30*(2), 47–71. Retrieved April 18, 2021, from http://www.jstor.org/stable/43442344

Hutchison, A. (2016). Writing center mission statement analysis. Retrieved from https://allisonhutchison.github.io.

Part 3

Measuring and Communicating Progress

7   Needs Assessment

Performing a needs assessment should be an early step in the process of establishing your writing center. A primary purpose of the embedded workplace model is to truly understand the local context and conventions that impact employees' day-to-day writing. Take the time to understand the mindsets with which employees approach their work, as well as what support they are actually interested in receiving. Some of these concepts and questions are covered in Chapter 4, and may be equally helpful to you here.

Initial Needs Assessment

Designing a writing center around the needs of your workplace helps to maximize the center's efficiency and your stakeholders' receptiveness. As a part of mapping the workplace (again, see Chapter 4), you should have asked questions about writers' needs and challenges, as well as about managers' frustrations and expectations. Many of these questions focused on what areas of writing were frustrating or challenging for writers (and later reviewers). But it is also important to investigate writers' beliefs and attitudes around writing and writing improvement.

Understanding employees' sense of confidence, self-efficacy, and locus of control is important to investigate before delving too deeply into training design (Arvind & Israrul Haque, 2008). Even the most brilliantly designed writing workshops and consultations will have limited effectiveness if the workplace is full of disengaged or demotivated employees. In some cases, the first step to establishing a center will be to address the sense of self-efficacy employees have in being able to improve their skills with the new resources (Arvind & Israrul Haque, 2008, p. 97).

It is also important to determine several aspects of the workplace environment, be it through observation, asking questions, or a more formal survey. As you likely know, writing center professionals are no strangers when it comes to integrating themselves into new environments and working with writing that deals with outside expertise. Writing center tutors are taught to think on their feet and to be *bricoleurs*, combining a number of different tutoring methods, available resources, and technologies to meet an individual's needs

DOI: 10.4324/9781003212959-11

(Yergeau, Wozniak, & Vandenberg, 2008). In a workplace environment, this means more than just thinking through individuals' preferred learning styles. It means understanding the everyday specifics of how we can reach our writers and earn their trust. Perhaps your workplace's writing involves restricted or confidential materials, which may impact your approach to earning writers' trust. Perhaps a disruption in work—be it routine building construction or a global pandemic—has dispersed your workforce. No matter what challenges arise, it's important to continually assess what writers are facing and how you can best meet them where they are. Each workplace and set of circumstances is unique, and each will require asking different questions to better understand employees' experiences.

Ongoing Needs Assessment

An initial needs assessment's value is not relegated to the introductory phases of a workplace writing center. These data can help you to see the ways in which writers have grown and changed. And, as most writing center professionals already know, it is important that we are constantly ready to defend and support our work. An important exercise is to speak with leaders in other departments about how they measure and communicate the value of their work. Some important questions to consider may include the following:

- How do you measure the impact of your work? Are stakeholders interested in hearing testimonial feedback? Are they only interested in quantitative data?
- What stakeholders are interested in hearing this information?
- Do stakeholders appreciate a very high-level overview of progress on paper? Do they prefer regular in-person chats?
- How often do you collect these progress measures? How often do you communicate them?
- What methods have you found helpful to support both short-term and long-term progress?
- How do you ensure that depicting success does not interfere with the actual purpose and function of the unit?
- Are there any measures that need to be taken to protect these data and/or those providing feedback?

It is likely you'll want to keep your immediate supervisor informed of progress and/or any issues on an ad hoc and quarterly basis. But you may also deliver a high-level overview to executive leadership or other stakeholders during events such as a year-end review, a request for more resources, or an explanation of new initiatives. Each workplace will be different, and these are important questions and strategies to consider in any new environment.

Sample Needs Assessment

Here I will include two sample needs assessment surveys, similar to those that I have used in the past within different workplaces. Please read Chapter 9 for more on surveys, especially as you consider what anonymity you can offer respondents and how you can use these data more specifically.

The first survey is a Writer Needs Assessment, designed to get a picture of what writers need and believe when it comes to their writing. The second is a Manager Needs Assessment, which should be distributed to those who generally supervise (and possibly train) the writers in your workplace. Following these surveys, I'll present reasons for their structure and what you can do with the resulting data.

Writer Needs Assessment

Respondent Profile
1. How long (cumulatively) have you worked at [Workplace Name]?
_____ years
2. How long have you been in the workforce?
_____ years
3. Is English your first language?
❏ Yes ❏ No
4. Which role best describes your current position? [List major functions, such as subject matter experts, analysts, etc.]

Attitude Inventory
5. I think writing is important in my current role.
Disagree ❏   ❏   ❏   ❏   ❏ Agree
6. I am confident in the quality of my writing.
Disagree ❏   ❏   ❏   ❏   ❏ Agree
7. I understand what my manager wants from me in terms of my writing.
Disagree ❏   ❏   ❏   ❏   ❏ Agree
8. I feel comfortable approaching my manager for writing feedback.
Disagree ❏   ❏   ❏   ❏   ❏ Agree
9. I feel comfortable approaching a peer for writing feedback.
Disagree ❏   ❏   ❏   ❏   ❏ Agree
10. I believe writing performance is a factor considered in promotions.
Disagree ❏   ❏   ❏   ❏   ❏ Agree
11. When I recognize a weakness in my skillset, I feel I have the ability to make improvements.
Disagree ❏   ❏   ❏   ❏   ❏ Agree

12. I feel that I am in an environment that supports my success.
Disagree ☐ ☐ ☐ ☐ ☐ Agree

13. When I recognize a weakness in my skillset, I feel I have the ability to make improvements.
Disagree ☐ ☐ ☐ ☐ ☐ Agree

14. I feel that I am in an environment that supports my success.
Disagree ☐ ☐ ☐ ☐ ☐ Agree

15. I believe my manager would be supportive of me attending writing training.
Disagree ☐ ☐ ☐ ☐ ☐ Agree

16. I would be willing to use Writing Center resources or attend a writing training session.
Disagree ☐ ☐ ☐ ☐ ☐ Agree

17. Which skills do you feel you could improve?
☐ Organization ☐ Tone ☐ Style
☐ Support/Analysis ☐ Clarity ☐ Grammar

Resources and Feedback

18. Please rank-order the following resources according to your interest in them (1= most interested, 5 = least interested).
☐ Writing style guide ☐ In-person writing workshops
☐ One-on-one writing consultations ☐ Online writing modules
☐ Remote writing workshops

19. I have enough time to carefully review my writing before submitting it.
Disagree ☐ ☐ ☐ ☐ ☐ Agree

20. I look carefully at final revisions made to documents that I have submitted.
Disagree ☐ ☐ ☐ ☐ ☐ Agree

21. In my [unit/area/team/department], it seems more important to meet deadlines than to spend more time writing and revising.
Disagree ☐ ☐ ☐ ☐ ☐ Agree

22. I feel that I receive an adequate amount of writing feedback from my manager or other reviewers.
Disagree ☐ ☐ ☐ ☐ ☐ Agree

23. I feel that I receive writing feedback from my manager or other reviewers in a timely manner.
Disagree ☐ ☐ ☐ ☐ ☐ Agree

24. Open-Ended: Please share any additional thoughts related to your writing, available/potential resources, and/or difficulties you've experienced.

Manager Needs Assessment

Respondent Profile

1. How long (cumulatively) have you worked at [Workplace Name]?
_____ years

2. How long have you been in the workforce?
_____ years

3. How many years did you work at [Workplace Name] before becoming a manager?
_____ years

4. Is English your first language?
❑ Yes ❑ No

Attitude Inventory

5. I think writing is an important skill for my staff.
Disagree ❑ ❑ ❑ ❑ ❑ Agree

6. Poor writing performance could compromise my willingness to recommend someone for a promotion.
Disagree ❑ ❑ ❑ ❑ ❑ Agree

7. If a report comes to me poorly written, it is my job to fix it.
Disagree ❑ ❑ ❑ ❑ ❑ Agree

8. If a report comes to me poorly written, it is the writer's job to fix it.
Disagree ❑ ❑ ❑ ❑ ❑ Agree

9. I believe I should spend more time reviewing report content than report writing quality.
Disagree ❑ ❑ ❑ ❑ ❑ Agree

10. I currently spend more time reviewing report content than report writing quality.
Disagree ❑ ❑ ❑ ❑ ❑ Agree

11. I am more interested in staff meeting deadlines than in taking additional time to improve report quality.
Disagree ❑ ❑ ❑ ❑ ❑ Agree

Resources and Feedback

12. I would be interested in a way to refer specific staff members to writing resources.
Disagree ❑ ❑ ❑ ❑ ❑ Agree

13. I would be supportive of a staff member attending writing training.
Disagree ❑ ❑ ❑ ❑ ❑ Agree

14. I would want to be notified when a staff member takes advantage of writing resources and classes.

Disagree ❑   ❑   ❑   ❑   ❑ Agree

15. I have an adequate amount of time to give feedback on staff's written products.

Disagree ❑   ❑   ❑   ❑   ❑ Agree

16. I have appropriate channels in place to provide feedback on staff's written products.

Disagree ❑   ❑   ❑   ❑   ❑ Agree

17. I believe my staff look at the feedback I provide them and learn from it.

Disagree ❑   ❑   ❑   ❑   ❑ Agree

18. Please rank-order the following writing skills in order of what you would like to see your staff improve (1 = most important to improve, 6 = least important to improve).

❑ Organization ❑ Tone ❑ Style

❑ Support/Analysis ❑ Clarity ❑ Grammar

19. Please rank-order the following resources according to your interest in their availability to your staff (1 = most interested, 5 = least interested).

❑ Writing style guide ❑ In-person writing workshops

❑ One-on-one writing consultations ❑ Online writing modules

❑ Remote writing workshops

20. Open-Ended: Please share any additional thoughts related to your staff's writing, the difficulties they've experienced, or available/potential resources.

Assessment Breakdown

The Writer Needs Assessment and Manager Needs Assessment are comprised of a few basic components: *Respondent Profile, Attitude Inventory,* and *Resources and Feedback.* When administering these assessments to writers and managers, it is best to remove the component labels to avoid influencing responses. However, they have been labeled here for your understanding.

Respondent Profile. The Respondent Profile will allow you to look at cross sections of data in your workplace. Asking about the respondent's specific role or team can help you see if writers' attitudes and support vary across these areas. You may also find a correlation between responses and how long respondents have been immersed in the workplace (or in the workforce overall). The question about whether English is the respondent's first language may also help you to identify additional or diverging forms of support that particularly interest multilingual writers. There may be other questions you wish to add to this section of your assessment; just be sure to consider what information the respondents will feel comfortable divulging, and how (or if) you can assure their anonymity.

Attitude Inventory. The Attitude Inventory is an opportunity for you to learn more about respondents' attitudes toward and beliefs about writing. These can not only be viewed through the cross sections of data provided by the Respondent Profile, but similar questions and answers can be compared between the Writer Needs Assessment and the Manager Needs Assessment. For example, you may find that writers underestimate the importance that managers put on their writing. Or you may find that managers believe their teams don't take the time to look at provided feedback, but that writers *are* looking at feedback—it just hasn't been helpful. You can also learn more about whether writers feel a sense of confidence in their writing and if they have any sense of self-efficacy when it comes to improving their skills. I have developed some of these questions based on common complaints and requests that I've heard while interviewing managers and writers at different organizations. If you interviewed your colleagues while laying the groundwork for your writing center, you may have additional ideas for questions in this assessment component.

The data from the Attitude Inventory can also be used as a benchmark against which you can measure progress. For instance, if you administer the survey again a year (or a few years) later, you can see if writers report higher levels of confidence in their writing, or if managers report lower levels of frustration. In subsequent years, you can add a question to the Respondent Profile about how frequently the respondent has used the writing center. This addition will allow you to see how results may differ between those who have taken advantage of the writing center and those who have not. In my own experience, I've been able to show that those who use a workplace writing center report higher levels of confidence in their writing—hopefully you'll have equally positive results to show for your efforts in time, too!

Resources and Feedback. The Resources and Feedback component is designed to reveal what support your colleagues are already using and recommending. You may prefer to break the Resources and Feedback component into two separate categories, depending on how many related questions you'd like to ask. Customize questions to your unique work environment in order to collect the most relevant data possible. For example, if your colleagues have mentioned existing writing resources that they like to use, you could ask respondents to check off which they use regularly. This could provide insight into the types of resources that are preferred, or whether your colleagues are turning to conflicting sources of advice. You may also ask more specifically about the feedback policies and processes within your workplace, to gauge current feelings toward them and what changes may be needed.

Additional Sections. You may find it helpful to build additional components into your needs assessments—just be sure to keep it brief enough that respondents are willing to complete it! You'll notice that both the Writer

Needs Assessment and Manager Needs Assessment end with an open-ended question. In my experience, many people tend to skip these, but it is important to give respondents additional space to voice any thoughts or concerns that you may not have anticipated. Even one or two valuable responses is usually worth the extra question. Additionally, you can include information for how respondents can get in touch with further questions and/or feedback after the survey is completed.

Summary

The data you collect from a needs assessment survey can help guide your writing center in a successful direction. Results can help you determine what services to prioritize and where to target your outreach. Administering needs assessments early in the process of starting your writing center will also help you to establish benchmarks that you can later measure against.

It's also important to be transparent with your colleague throughout the needs assessment process. Collecting these data ultimately benefits the respondents, but in many workplaces, people are uncomfortable putting feedback in writing. More best practices will be covered in Chapter 9.

References

Arvind, M., & Israrul Haque, M. (July 2008). Impact of locus of control, trainer's effectiveness, & training design on learning. *Indian Journal of Industrial Relations, 44*(1), 89–98.

Yergeau, M., Wozniak, K., & Vandenberg, P. (2008). Expanding the space of f2f: Writing centers and audio-visual-textual conferencing. *Kairos, 13*(1). Retrieved from http://kairos.technorhetoric.net/13.1/topoi/yergeau-et-al/

8 Data Logs

Keeping records of completed consultations is a common practice in writing centers, and a workplace writing center should be no exception. From the very first day your writing center is operating, you should have a place and procedure for collecting consultation information. These data can be used to measure your outreach, trends over time, consistency of consultants' approaches, and relevant information to be communicated to stakeholders. This chapter will help you think through what data to collect, where to house these data, and how to report (and protect!) these data.

Useful Data

When a student enters an academic writing center, it's typical for them to have to fill out a tutoring form or to answer a few questions at a check-in desk. These questions often encompass their year in school, what type of assignment they're working on, and what the related course code is. This allows writing center directors to track which students are using the writing center, as well as if there is any correlation with student retention rate. Both of these measures can be useful in appealing to university stakeholders for budgetary needs.

What to Consider Tracking

In your workplace writing center, you'll need to think carefully about what information could help demonstrate your impact and make an impression on relevant stakeholders. You'll want to collect enough data to draw conclusions, but not so much that writers find intake forms tedious or invasive. You may have writers submit information in advance of a consultation—for instance, as part of a form while they are booking a time slot. Writing consultants can also collect this information when a writer shows up (in person or remotely) for their session. I've found the following information to be useful to collect from writers when they engage with the writing center:

- Desired consultation time and length (30- and 60-minute blocks work well)
- Title/Role (e.g., specialist, analyst, intern, manager)

DOI: 10.4324/9781003212959-12

- Assignment (e.g., formal report, memo, white paper)
- Desired focus for session (e.g., organization, tone, style)
- Desired session type (face-to-face, video, phone)
- Whether or not this is their first session

There may be other relevant questions that make sense in your unique context; for instance, you may want to know if a writer was referred by anyone. Be consistent in collecting this information, keeping data logs as complete and as accurate as possible. If you'd like to save your writer some questions to answer, you could also consider having the writing consultant fill out the writer's role after the session. Many workplaces have internal directories that would allow consultants to double-check this information. Depending on how you set up your consultation request forms/systems, you may have the option to auto-populate some of these fields, too.

Writing consultants should also record relevant data after the session, including:

- Total length of session
- Issues addressed in the session (e.g., tone, clarity, grammar)
- General notes on the content of the session

Later in this chapter, I'll provide more detail about how you can use this information as you establish baseline and ongoing metrics. The outlier here is the section for notes that your consultant should fill out immediately following each writing consultation.

Consultation Notes

Also a common practice in academic writing centers, providing a data field for consultants to reflect upon and record their interaction with a writer serves a number of purposes. First, it helps consultants to grow in and learn from their experiences; it also provides a space to note any important details that fall outside of the limited form options. Second, session descriptions are useful when a consultant is working with the same writer repeatedly over time. Consultants can look back at previous sessions to remind themselves what they worked on last time with the same writer. They can scaffold on this information, building the writer's knowledge without being too repetitive. And third...session notes just offer an additional layer of accountability and protection for the writing center. Though these notes are intended only for the writing center to reference internally, they can be helpful if a conflict arises later. I have occasionally worked with writers who later misrepresent the content of a writing consultation. For instance, a writer may run out of time to make revisions and tell their manager that the writing center suggested no revisions, placing the blame on the consultant. In order to preserve the writing center's reputation, you may have to clarify what was covered in

Sample Consultation Form

Writer

Name: _____ Title/Job Role: _____

Session Date: _____ Session Time (30 or 60 minutes): _____

Is this your first consultation with the Writing Center?

❑ Yes ❑ No

Select the item that best describes what we'll be working on:

❑ Report ❑ Memo ❑ Email

❑ Article ❑ Proposal ❑ Presentation

❑ Performance Assessment ❑ Other: _____

When is this item due? _____

What issues would you like to address? Select all that apply.

❑ Organization ❑ Tone ❑ Style

❑ Support/Analysis ❑ Clarity ❑ Grammar

❑ Unsure ❑ Other: _____

What type of meeting would you prefer?

❑ Face-to-face ❑ Video ❑ Phone Call

If you would like a writing consultant to review your work in advance of your session, please attach a copy to this form. Please direct any other comments or questions to [contact].

Consultant

Consultant Name: _____ Length of Consultation (minutes): _____

What did you work on in the session?

❑ Organization ❑ Tone ❑ Style

❑ Support/Analysis ❑ Clarity ❑ Grammar

Notes: _____

_____

the session—not betraying the writer's trust by sharing the full notes (unless absolutely necessary), but by sharing what issues the consultant recorded talking about.

In session notes, consultants can also share any frustrating experiences that they have had with a writer. They may wish to note if a writer was resistant to feedback or stated that the writing center's advice contradicted a manager's. All consultants should be sure to use respectful language within these notes. Though they are not intended to be shared beyond the writing center, extenuating possibilities could make them more public (e.g., a writer misrepresents the consultation experience to a manager). As long as writers keep their notes objective and respectful, this should not raise further issues.

Housing and Protecting Data

Ideally, consultants will log information from each consultation on the day it has occurred, and you'll return to this inventory periodically to pull relevant information. The database software available to each workplace will vary, but it doesn't need to be complex. Select a platform that can be accessed remotely by consultants, either as a document on a shared drive (e.g., an Excel spreadsheet) or as a cloud-based online service (e.g., a Google sheet). Using privacy controls or password protection, ensure that only currently employed writing consultants can access these logs. Additionally, ensure that there is a back-up copy available, or set up automated back-up processes. Collaborate with your workplace's IT team to establish best practices.

Using Data Effectively

Your data won't speak for itself—you'll have to carefully consider what you can learn from the information you're collecting, and to think about what will interest different stakeholders.

Quarterly and Year-End Updates

Analyzing data logs and generating reports should be a routine habit for your writing center. These metrics can act as snapshots of your progress over time, developing a bigger picture about your writing center's impact and reach. Quarterly reports can be a helpful reflection point for writing consultants, while year-end reports can be particularly useful when updating executive stakeholders or leadership groups.

One of the simplest metrics you can pull from your data log is the number of sessions held in the writing center for a given period of time. Look at how many consultations have been completed in each quarter, as well as how year-end totals compare. Ideally, you will see that the writing center's popularity and demand have grown over its years of operation. But you can also identify busy times of year for the writing center. If you know that demand for sessions lulls over the summer, for instance, you can plan to tackle other projects during that time. And if you know when to anticipate surges in use, you can better prepare consultants for a busy season.

Tracking the number of consultations that your writing center completes can also help you to strategize for future demand and potential expansion. When you see jumps in the number of sessions each consultant is handling, it's time to think about if and when you'll need to hire an additional consultant. Proving the increase in demand is helpful when you need to approach workplace leadership to request additional hires or resources.

In addition to looking at the total number and distribution of sessions over time, you can break this data down by individual writers. Tracking how many individual writers you've helped in a period of time—or even how many new writers you've attracted to the writing center for their first visit—can tell you more about your reach within the workplace. You can (and should) also look at writer return rates. In other words, look to see what percentage of writers return to the writing center for another consultation. You could limit this measure to a period of time, but generally, knowing how many people are willing to return to the writing center as a total percentage is helpful. A high rate of return (as long as sessions are voluntary) indicates that writers trust writing consultants and find value in your services.

When presenting updates to executive leadership, keep your reports brief and high-level. Focus on the growth and breadth of your impact, and use this information to support any appeals for budget increases or resources. Best practices will vary between different workplaces, but generally you should plan to provide an annual update to executive leadership. Learn when decisions are made about the budget that impacts your writing center, and be sure to offer these updates in advance of any important deadlines.

Strategic Outreach

The data that you collect as you log completed consultations can also help you to advertise writing center services more effectively. In my experience, if a writer submits a document in advance of a session (and if the document is fewer than ten pages), a consultation will average about 20 minutes in length. There will certainly be exceptions to this average—some writers have more serious errors to correct, or may wish to spend more time asking questions. But sharing the average session length can help you show potential writing center users that the time commitment is even lower than they may expect. In any case, it gives them an idea of what to expect if they use your services. If your writing center has enjoyed high rates of return, you can also use this figure to promote your services. It can also help writers see that writing centers are a resource designed for ongoing, repeated use.

In the Sample Consultation Form (p. 101), you'll notice that writers are asked to share their role or title in the workplace. You may add an additional field (or modify this field) to ask what department or unit the writer is in. Collecting this information will allow you to see who is using the writing center—and who is not. Perhaps you will see that your writing center serves a lot of managers and higher-ranking staff; sharing these statistics can help combat any assumptions that the writing center is a remedial service. Perhaps you will see that there is a particular team or unit that is not using the writing center. This may indicate that you should check in with the writers in this area. There are a number of reasons why a particular unit may avoid the writing center, including but not limited to:

- A manager discouraging use of the writing center
- Lack of awareness about writing center services
- Assumptions that the writing center cannot help with their particular work
- Worries that the writing center cannot work around fast-paced deadlines
- Assumptions that the writing center cannot view sensitive material

By speaking with writers and management in areas that you're not reaching, you may be able to better understand their relationship to the writing center. You can clear up misconceptions, invite them specifically to use services, and even consider offering writing workshops that relate to their area of work. You can identify advocates within these business lines if a few people have used the writing center, and you can prioritize your outreach efforts to persuade these teams.

Meaningful Trends and Support

If you have been capturing the issues covered in writing center consultations, you can also develop a picture of what writing challenges your colleagues face. Because the writing center is meant to offer individualized instruction, you should ideally see a range of issues covered in consultations. When your writing center launches, however, you may find that some issues receive much more focus than others. You may find that writers are insisting on tackling grammar in their sessions, but that over time you are able to convince them to consider holistic issues such as organization and clarity. You may alternately find that there are major issues with these holistic issues, and that many writers need to focus on organization or analysis before they can move on to anything else. Over time, the shifts you see in the focus of sessions can help you determine if your workplace has been able to redirect or evenly distribute focus between different writing components.

If you find that a large portion of writing consultations are focused on a particular issue—let's say, for example, tone—you can think about how to strategically support writers. A consultant could put together a one-page resource about best practices related to tone, or record a video module with some tricks and tips for ensuring appropriate tone. You could also offer a workshop focused on tone, inviting writers to come and discuss issues and practice skills together. On the other hand, if you find that a large portion of writing consultations are focused on grammar, you may need to revisit the center's messaging and marketing strategies. It may be a good time to clarify that the writing center is not a copyediting service, but is designed to help writers tackle a wide range of challenges.

It's also a good idea to periodically review the spread of issues that each consultant is covering within their sessions. You may find that different consultants favor different issues, in which case you'll want to address this and keep it in check. Newer or less confident consultants may limit their focus to lower-order issues such as grammar and style formatting, while more seasoned consultants focus on high-order issues. Keep an eye on changes over time and major shifts in focus between consultants. Pointing out the overall areas of focus and what different consultants tend to bring up in sessions can help them to be more critical of their practices. You may also encourage consultants to take a look at the session log themselves to calculate what issues they spend the most time focusing on, reminding them to be conscious of this over time.

Summary

It can't be emphasized enough: Start tracking meaningful data from the writing center's very first day. Keeping a log of completed consultations will provide you with valuable insight into your writing center's focus, impact, and changes over time. Revisit these data periodically, generating internal reports for your team every quarter. Provide major stakeholders and executive leadership with high-level data annually; be strategic in your timing if you have specific budget requests in mind. Be sure to maintain your data and reports so that the information is complete, accurate, accessible to your team, and protected from other viewers.

Carefully consider what data will hold meaning for your stakeholders at various levels. This will determine what information you need to collect before, during, and after consultations. It can also help you think through what trends to watch for and what metrics will help support your center's growth and development. Though you certainly don't want to overwhelm writers by asking for too much information, ensuring that you collect and maintain comprehensive data sets will benefit your writing center in the long run.

9 Surveys

Surveys are a classic method for collecting both qualitative and quantitative data about your writing center, as alluded to in Chapters 4 and 7. Many resources already exist for building writing center surveys, so this chapter will focus on considerations specific to workplace writing centers. I highly recommend the following three texts for more comprehensive information on writing center research methods and survey design:

- Babcock, R. D., & Thonus, T. (2018). *Researching the writing center: Towards an evidence-based practice.* 2nd ed. Peter Lang Publishing, Inc.
- Grutsch McKinney, J. (2016). *Strategies for writing center research.* Anderson: Parlor Press.
- Schendel, E., & Macauley, W. J. (2012). *Building writing center assessments that matter.* Utah State UP.

Though the listed texts are written for academic writing center contexts, their guidance will still apply in most cases.

Setting Up Your Survey

Let's follow some common advice shared in writing centers: *Consider your audience.* Who is it that you need to hear from, and what might motivate them to respond? How will you be using resulting data, and how can you ethically collect it? Through every step of the surveying process, be sure to respect your potential respondents and have well-thought-out procedures.

Respecting Your Respondents

Any time you ask respondents to share their opinions, experiences, or data, you risk placing them in a position of vulnerability. This is especially true in a high-stakes environment like a workplace. If, for example, you ask writers to rate how satisfied they are with their managers' feedback, they may understandably worry about whether managers will be able to access this information and/or if their responses will be tied to their identity. If respondents don't feel that they can trust you to protect their responses, they are

DOI: 10.4324/9781003212959-13

likely to ignore your request for feedback or to provide inaccurate data when self-reporting.

Consider whether you can reasonably offer respondents anonymity. Even if you aren't asking respondents to include their names, they may still be identifiable based on their combination of responses to questions. For instance, if a respondent reports that they work in a small unit and they have been employed at your workplace for two years, their identity may immediately be apparent even without a name. In such a case, you may need to explain to potential respondents—within the actual survey or when distributing it—how the collected data will be used. Anonymity may be a complex or overreaching promise to offer potential respondents, but you can take measures to ensure that responses remain as confidential as possible. You may mention how the data will be protected (e.g., on a protected drive or with a password) or that response sets will only be viewed by the writing center. In the latter case, this assures respondents that their managers will not be able to rifle through individual responses; instead, managers will hear summary data about general trends within larger populations.

Additionally, be empathetic to the time and energy that surveys demand from respondents. When you distribute your survey, provide an estimated amount of time that the survey will take to complete. Depending on the survey length, you may want to mention whether respondents will be able to pause, save, and return to complete the survey or whether they will need to complete it in one sitting. If your survey is hosted online, look into whether you can display a progress bar so that respondents don't become frustrated and exit prematurely. Think, too, about how much time *you* might be willing to spend on a similar survey from another department. I have found that if I design surveys to take fewer than ten minutes (and if I communicate this fact), more individuals are likely to respond. Survey fatigue is real—if you are already embedded in the workplace where your writing center is (or will be) hosted, you likely already know this. Pay attention to when other workplace teams send out surveys and try to target a different time frame, so as not to overwhelm your potential respondents.

Be sure to investigate whether your workplace has an internal board or representative who oversees human subject research. Some workplaces (especially larger ones) have established processes and paperwork for the collection, management, and reporting of data. This function may not be as clearly marked as it would be in an academic setting, where you can more easily find Institutional Review Boards. You may need to inquire through departments such as Human Resources or Legal. It's also possible that your workplace does not have established procedures at all, but it's best to do your due diligence beforehand rather than risk your data (and reputation!) afterward. Whether or not you need formal approval to survey your colleagues, you should still think carefully about informed consent. Respondents should clearly understand how their responses will be used and how their participation will or will not impact them. For more sensitive projects, this may involve a writer's electronic or handwritten signature. For many surveys, you can simply include language on the first page (or within the body of an email) that explains that if a respondent chooses to submit responses, they are consenting for the data to be used for specified purposes.

Surveying Procedures

One of the first steps in developing a survey is to consider what platform you will use to collect data. Your workplace may have access to survey software that can be used internally; if not, there are an abundance of online survey websites that you can use. Be aware that online survey sites commonly offer only select features for free—you may only be able to save a certain number of responses or compile a limited number of questions. Ask your workplace in advance if you can purchase an account, or if you can access an existing corporate account.

Sometimes, the simplest method is best. I've found that sharing paper surveys at the end of in-person workshops elicits a greater number of responses than emailing participants afterward with a survey link. In these cases, the additional step of data entry is worth it for a more complete data set. Whether you end up using a paper-based or digital method to collect survey responses, you'll need to consider what question format options you'll need and what data privacy measures you'll have to follow. Whether you're password protecting an online survey account or keeping paper surveys locked up until they can be shredded, it's important to take every measure to protect your respondents' information.

Timing is another consideration for your survey. Perhaps you've already identified a time of year when potential respondents aren't already inundated with survey requests, but you'll also need to consider your data collection window. As a starting point, I typically recommend two weeks for data collection. Sending a reminder at the beginning of the second week will allow you to reach colleagues who may have been out of office the previous week, while two emails in a two-week span shouldn't feel too burdensome for recipients. If you work in a day-shift environment and are notifying potential respondents by email, you may want to send your message late at night or early in the morning so that it's at the top of everyone's inbox when they sign on. If your work environment follows a typical weekday schedule, you may want to avoid distributing a survey on a Monday or Friday, when people may be busiest or most inclined to take a day off.

Distributing paper surveys in person provides a fairly straightforward opportunity to explain context and answer questions, but in most cases, you'll likely share surveys digitally. The following are some best practices for email distribution.

- Provide some context for the survey in the body of your email, but keep the message brief enough to keep the recipient's attention. Lengthy details can be provided as attachments.

- Use the blind copy (BCC) function to send the survey out to a large group of people, which will prevent a flood of "reply-all" responses.
- Consider individually emailing respondents and addressing them by name if you have the time and staff to do so.
- Clearly link to the survey in the email, if possible.
- Provide contact information so that recipients can get in touch with additional questions.

You may also think about how you can motivate people to respond. With a more important survey (for instance, a five-year benchmark survey) you could consider raffling off a gift card to a survey respondent. But more simply, you can include a line in the email that explains how filling the survey out as completely as possible will benefit the respondent—even if you're just mentioning that their feedback is valuable and will lead to an improvement in the services they use.

Example Survey Email

Here is a sample email that you can adapt for your particular research, situation, and individual workplace. You'll notice that the text is fairly brief, but is focused on informed consent and motivating the recipient to complete the survey. A potential respondent would know what to expect when they click on the link, the amount of time it will take to complete, and how their data may be used.

Hello, [Name or Participant Group],

Strong writing and clear communication are vital to the work that we do. For the past [#] years, the Writing Center has sought to support you in this important task—now, we're trying to learn more about what has been helpful and what we can do to improve our services and resources.

Please take the [Name of Survey, hyperlinked], which will ask questions about your writing habits, preferences, challenges, and improvements. No information will be gathered that could personally identify you. While your participation is voluntary and you can exit the survey at any point, your input is greatly appreciated and will guide the way we continue to serve [participant group].

Your response should take less than [#] minutes to record, and should be submitted by [date].

Thanks in advance for your time and consideration. Please reach out to [name] at [contact information] if you have any questions.

Sincerely,

[Name and contact information]

[Writing Center affiliation]

Surveys That Can Support Your Work

One of the first types of surveys likely to support your work is a needs assessment, as explored in Chapter 7. A needs assessment survey not only allows you to establish benchmarks but also allows you to survey the same populations later on to measure changes and trends over time. Depending on the demographic information that you collect within this type of survey, you can compare responses between different levels (e.g., managers vs. staff), changes in attitudes over time (e.g., report reviewer frustration a few years ago vs. now), and impact of different variables (e.g., the reported confidence of writers who use the writing center vs. who do not).

Post-Consultation Feedback Surveys

Another common survey in writing center work is a post-consultation feedback survey. This is a survey sent (or handed) to writers immediately after they've completed a consultation with the writing center. This feedback can help your team to see where the perceived strengths and weaknesses of your services lie. In a post-consultation feedback survey, you might ask writers to rate or assess the following components.

- How satisfied they are with the…
  - Ease of the appointment-scheduling process
  - Quality of the consultation itself
  - Convenience of the session/service
  - Length of the consultation

- Whether they feel…
  - That their concerns were fully addressed, partially addressed, or not addressed
  - More confident, equally confident, or less confident in their writing

- The likelihood that they will…
  - Return to the writing center again in the future
  - Refer someone else to the writing center

Consider, too, collecting a bit of information about the session itself—for instance, whether it was the writer's first consultation with the writing center, or what type of written project they were working on. This may help you to identify discrepancies in responses between different types of consultations. And as with most surveys, you may want to add an open-ended question or two. Ask writers what improvements or changes they would like to see made to the writing consultation process. You may also ask for general feedback, where respondents can write any further concerns or points of praise.

You may find it advantageous to send out this survey every time a consultation is completed with the writing center, especially when your writing center is first launching. However, as you establish relationships with writing center users, you may shift your strategy—otherwise, those who repeatedly use the writing center and complete surveys will skew your data. A better strategy over time may be to administer a post-consultation survey whenever a writer completes their first-ever consultation with the writing center. As your writing center grows busier and more established, you can also switch to a more randomized distribution model. For instance, each quarter you may randomly select 1 in every 5 writing center users to complete a feedback survey. Your approach will depend on how many people your writing center serves, the size of your workplace, how established the writing center is, and what data you are collecting.

Workshop Surveys

Similar to post-consultation feedback surveys, you may want to distribute surveys right after writers have attended a workshop. You may collect some of the same data as you would after a consultation (e.g., their confidence level, their likelihood of using the service again), but you may also add or modify questions. The following are questions that can be useful when gathering workshop-related feedback.

- How satisfied they are with the...

  - Format of the workshop
  - Amount of examples provided
  - Time allotted for hands-on practice
  - Length of the full workshop
  - Workshop content
  - Workshop presenter

- Whether they now know more about...

  - [List skills or concepts covered within workshop]

- If a virtual workshop, how they feel about...

  - How easy it was to see/hear the presenter
  - Accessing relevant technology (e.g., polls, interactive functions)
  - Streaming quality
  - Level of engagement with workshop material and other participants

Administering these types of postworkshop surveys can help your team learn how to better market and design workshops for different populations in your workplace. In the past, similar surveys have helped me to better pace my workshops so that attendees find them more engaging, convenient, and worth their time. And if you find that a high percentage of workshop attendees would, say, recommend the workshop to a colleague, this is a great figure to use in future marketing!

Limitations

Though surveys are a great tool to have in your arsenal, you should be aware of their limitations. Because you are inviting people to voluntarily share their thoughts and opinions, you are more likely to hear from those who feel strongly on either end of the spectrum—in other words, you'll hear less from those who are neutral and hear from those who were very pleased and those who were very frustrated. In my own experience, I've seen data that skew very favorably for the writing center, with users reporting positive experiences. While this is encouraging, I also keep in mind that people who voluntarily use writing center services *and* who take the time to provide feedback are those who likely already feel positive about professional development opportunities. I've seen data become further skewed positive when the same repeat writing center users complete the feedback survey more than once. Be aware of who you are engaging with your surveys, and what factors may impact the accuracy of the results.

Furthermore, any time that you are asking respondents to self-report their experiences, you risk biased responses. If a workshop attendee is asked to fill out a survey in the same room where the facilitator is standing, they may be inclined to record the answers that the facilitator wants to hear. Or, if a writer fills out the survey a few days later, their memory of the experience may be less accurate, affecting their responses.

Summary

Surveys are a well-established and easily recognized tool for collecting both qualitative and quantitative data. They can help you to establish point-in-time measurements when administered repeatedly, allowing you to track trends and shifts over time.

Designing surveys requires careful consideration for how the respondent will interact with the survey, as well as how the writing center (and relevant stakeholders) will use these data. Informed consent is a vital part of the surveying process, but it's also important to think about what time and energy the survey will demand from potential respondents. Respect respondents' time, privacy, and right to know what their participation really means. Whether you collect data through a web-based or paper-based platform, ensure that every measure is taken to protect respondents' personal information.

Surveys can be particularly helpful when you want to assess the impact of services like writing center consultations and workshops. By listening to feedback related to user experiences, the writing center can improve services and strengthen relationships with writers. Be aware that surveys have limitations, including inaccuracy in self-reporting and skewed data resulting from who does and does not respond. But when used in tandem with other measures of success, surveys are a worthwhile method that can yield valuable data.

10 Pretest/Posttest Quasi-Experiment

Though qualitative data are common in writing center work and study, quantitative data can be more compelling to certain stakeholders. In traditional (academic) writing centers, this may involve sharing graduation/retention rates among writing center users; of course, workplace writing centers need to think of different ways to prove their efficacy. Using a quasi-experimental approach is one way that your writing center can demonstrate improvement in writing quality, though it is a more time-consuming and complicated research method to use. It is also a method that becomes more plausible when your writing center has built a reputation in your workplace and has developed rapport with writers.

My own first attempt at a quasi-experimental research design came in my first few years of working for the Federal Reserve Bank of Philadelphia—I found out pretty quickly that while my colleagues found qualitative research interesting, what they *really* valued were numbers. Sure, leadership was pleased to hear that writing center users reported overall positive experiences, but they were more interested to know whether the department's quality of writing was improving as writers continued to engage with the writing center. In order to establish a measure of writing quality, I identified a pretest/posttest quasi-experiment as a strong method to pursue (Creswell & Creswell, 2018, p. 136; Lauer & Asher, 1988, p. 199). Simply put, this involved looking at two different drafts of the same piece of writing: The first would be the document that a writer brought to the writing center, while the second would be the version that the writer independently revised following the writing center session. By finding a way to assess the quality of these documents—as objectively as possible—I knew I could measure the impact of the writing consultation on the subsequent draft. Ultimately, I enlisted a panel of experts to help rate writing samples using an agreed-upon rubric.

The resulting study was more successful than I had anticipated, although I later added a number of improvements to the study design while writing my dissertation at Texas Tech University in 2019. In both iterations, I found that our writing center did have a statistically significant impact on all measured writing components. The results of the original study were covered in *Harvard Business Review*, an article that continues to connect me with those interested in establishing workplace writing centers (Bernoff, 2017). The 2017

DOI: 10.4324/9781003212959-14

article provides the specifics of what I did in this original study, but in the remainder of this chapter, I will provide a more general, step-by-step approach to how you can use a pretest/posttest quasi-experimental method to measure improvements in writing quality in your own workplace.

Writing Sample Selection

First, decide on what you're comparing as part of your pretest/posttest. You could consider comparing writing samples from the same writer over different periods of time, or you could replicate what I did at the Reserve Bank by looking at the impact of a writing center consultation on two different drafts. No matter what writing samples you choose to study, you will need to get informed consent from any participants. You may ask frequent writing center users if they are interested in sharing written drafts for a study that will help support the writing center. You may select department writers at random to ask if they are willing to participate in your study. Err on the side of asking more writers than you think you need—some will opt out, and some will provide samples that don't work well for this type of study. For instance, if you collect a number of memos, and one writer instead provides a recently written PowerPoint slide, it would be too easy for your raters to identify the PowerPoint slide drafts as belonging to the same writer. If you will be testing for significance, you will also want to have as large a sample set as possible (though not one that is too large for raters to complete without fatigue).

Assembling a Panel of Raters

The writing samples should be scored by people who are familiar with or set standards for written quality in your workplace, but not by those who have direct affiliation with the writing center, so as to avoid bias. Managers, report reviewers, and subject matter experts may make good candidates, especially if they have years of experience in writing at the same level as the sample writers. Using a panel of multiple raters will help you to establish rubric and scoring validity (Frey, Botan, & Kreps, 1999, p. 116), as well as to account for the subjective nature of writing (Shirotha, 2016, p. 111). I have found that three panel reviewers is a good number to recruit, but you may require a different number based on the size of your workplace and the diversity of viewpoints you want to represent.

Clearly communicate with your panel about the time commitment that will be necessary for your study. A strong pretest/posttest design may involve multiple conversations around rubric ratings, rubric definitions, and norming, on top of the time you are asking them to actually assess the samples.

Developing a Rubric

In order to keep scoring procedures consistent across your panelists, you'll need to agree upon a rubric, likely over several rounds of conversation (Saxton, Belanger, & Becker, 2012). Your categories may be informed by writing components that you track elsewhere in writing center processes, such as the issue categories in your consultation data log (e.g., organization, clarity, tone). Once you've determined the components you'll be assessing, you'll need to create a definition for each component so that the panelists have a shared understanding.

You will also need to create a quantifiable rating scale for the rubric—perhaps you will rate each writing component on a scale of 1 to 4, with a 1 being weakest and a 4 being strongest. You may need to come up with a more qualitative reference point for these numbers, as well. For instance, you may describe a "1" rating as "Unacceptable," where the reviewer would have to return the piece to the writer for a total rewrite, whereas a "2" rating would be described as "Needing Heavy Revisions" from the reviewer.

Consider whether you will accept half-point scores from your panelists, as well as whether you wish to weight some components as more important than others. For example, I have often halved the score for grammar and proofreading categories, since the higher-order issue scores (like supporting details, clarity) are more indicative of strong writing. Breaking the rubric into components allows the panel to take into account each sample's particular strengths and weaknesses, rather than assigning a singular, less reliable holistic score (East, 2009, p. 91).

Once you've identified the components you'll be assessing and the rating scales for assessment, you'll need to fill in the rubric. This involves specific definitions of what each component looks like at different rating points. Here is a basic template as an example, in which you would need to describe what each square would look like based on your workplace's writing.

Component	1 – Not acceptable	2 – Heavy revision	3 – Light revision	4 – No/Minimal revision required
Organization				
Supporting detail				
Clarity				
Grammar/proofreading				

As an example, perhaps the "Grammar/Proofreading – 3" box says "a few errors are present, but do not affect the reader's understanding" while the "Grammar/Proofreading – 4" box says "virtually no errors are present". You will need to decide what each component would look like at different levels within your own workplace; the descriptions should clearly represent a recognizable experience/product for the rating panel.

To recap, the process of developing a rubric should involve creating the following document drafts:

- A list of descriptions for each writing component
- A list of descriptions of each point category
- A rubric that demonstrates what each component looks like within each point category

Again, you will likely need to meet with your panel of raters more than once to agree upon any changes to the proposed three documents. Once all the raters are in agreement, you can move on to the next step: Norming to determine interrater reliability.

Norming

Although using a panel of evaluators helps provide some reliability to scoring procedures, it's important to make sure that the variance between scores is still fairly small (Hughes & Hayhoe, 2007, p. 62). In advance of the final scoring session, meet with the panel for a norming session. Select a few sample sets of writing that are typical of the full data set, and mix them up so that they're not collated by pair. If panelists see pre/post samples paired, it's possible that their scoring could be swayed by an attempt to identify which is which.

Before beginning the norming session, give a brief refresher of the agreed-upon rubric and definition sheet; provide copies of these along with the writing samples. Pay attention to how long it takes the panel to complete this process, as it will help you estimate how long evaluating the full set will take later on.

One way to determine interrater reliability is to use Cronbach's alpha coefficient (Lauer & Asher, 1988, p. 196; Minnich et al., 2018, p. 368). This test is commonly used "to yield a single consistency estimate of interrater reliability across multiple judges" (Stemler, 2004, p. 4). Cronbach's alpha coefficient provides a value between 0 and 1; researchers should aim for values between .7 and .9 (Creswell & Creswell, 2018, p. 154). If the value is outside of this target range, you'll need to revisit your scoring procedures and possibly even your panel. Is one rater coming up with wildly different numbers than the rest? If so, why? It's possible you'll need to have another discussion about the decided-upon rubric in order to clarify its consistent application and/or whether any of the definitions need to be modified. It's possible you may need to tweak the number of raters on your panel, or investigate further if a particular rater is straying far from the rest. If and when you do reach the targeted Cronbach's alpha coefficient value, you are ready to proceed to the full assessment process.

Assessment Process

When your panel is ready to assess the full set of samples, keep the conditions as similar as possible to those existing during the norming session. This may mean booking the same conference room to ensure similar levels of quiet, temperature, and light; it may mean encouraging raters to complete their review around the same time of day or on the same day of the week.

Blind the samples as much as possible. Remove any identifying information from the samples, including subject-specific terms that could clue evaluators in to the writer's identity (e.g., if writers have all been assigned to review different software products, use a generic term for the product itself).

Code your samples so that you can easily re-pair the sets later. One method is to use a random number generator and to mark a value on each sample set. You can either create a key of the numbers used in each sample set so that you can later pair them up again, or you can add a digit to the end of the number as an additional code (e.g., an odd digit for pretest sample and an even digit for posttest sample). Be sure to mix up the stacks of samples so that the pairs are separated in different halves of the full set; again, this is to try to keep evaluators from scoring a sample set too closely together.

Resulting Data

Once you've collected all of the scores from your panel, you'll need to analyze the data. First, use the codes on each sample to re-pair the presession and postsession scores assigned by each evaluator. Then, use any statistical software available to you to run a paired *t*-test. If you work for a larger organization, perhaps you can enlist the help of a quantitative analyst or statistician to help with this portion of the analysis (this is the route I've typically taken!). A paired *t*-test will allow you to examine differences between pretest and posttest scores (Frey et al., 1999, p. 345).

In a paired *t*-test, it is typical to check for a *p*-value lower than .05 to indicate a significant difference (at 95% confidence) between the two sets; your preferred parameters may differ, but this is a good guideline. A paired *t*-test should also yield the mean, standard error, standard deviation, degrees of freedom, lower and upper confidence intervals, *t*-value, and *p*-value. All of these can be used to frame your data set in different ways, but the *p*-value is what will show whether there is a statistically significant difference in score between the two samples. You can run this test for the overall rubric scores for the samples, as well as for each component within the rubric. For example, you can say that the overall writing quality improved, or you can point to specific changes in writing clarity, writing organization, and so on.

Hopefully, an ideal *p*-value will support the fact that working with your writing center improves the assessed quality of workplace writing. It is worth acknowledging that statistical significance "is on its own valueless", making up only a small part of the stories that you can tell about your writing center's impact (Ziliak & McCloskey, 2009, p. 2303).

It's also important to check again for interrater reliability, since this is a different assessment session than the norming session conducted earlier. Test again for Cronbach's alpha coefficient so that you can determine whether your data set displays sufficient interrater reliability.

Summary

Performing a pretest/posttest quasi-experiment requires time, resources, and careful analysis. It will likely take at least a few months to amass a set of appropriate writing samples, ensure adequate writer participation, develop a writing rubric, select and train a panel of raters, and actually analyze the set of scores. In my own experience, I have been able to use pretest/posttest quasi-experiments to provide quantitative support for writing centers' value in the workplace—but it is only one possible method of doing so, and it may not necessarily generate the desired outcome or type of data that makes sense for your workplace. But if the leadership at your workplace is particularly focused on metrics, and you have colleagues who are interested in participating in this type of research, it can be valuable route to pursue.

A pretest/posttest quasi-experiment like the one described in this chapter presents a unique scholarship opportunity for writing centers. Although it is possible to measure student performance in a classroom setting using similar methods (Nickerson, Rapanta, & Goby, 2017), it would be nearly impossible to do this as an academic writing center director. Traditional writing centers serve students from many different classrooms and disciplines; tutors see assignments that will be graded by many different instructors. In these cases, there is no way to measure what qualifies as "good" writing. Within a workplace department, however, it can be possible to point to department writing standards that govern good writing. Plus, a panel of assessment experts can be found in a pool of more experienced colleagues.

Exploring this gap in writing center research offers new avenues to scholars interested in this line of work. Furthermore, I hope that the forms of research possible in workplace writing center environments will help to add more legitimacy and recognition to the work that academic writing centers do.

References

Bernoff, J. (2017, February 21). Why your organization needs a writing center. *Harvard Business Review*. Retrieved from https://hbr.org/2017/02/why-your-organizationneeds-a-writing-center.

Creswell, J. W., & Creswell, J. D. (2018). *Research design: Qualitative, quantitative, and mixed methods approaches* (5th ed.). Los Angeles, CA: SAGE Publications, Inc.

East, M. (2009). Evaluating the reliability of a detailed analytic scoring rubric for foreign language writing. *Assessing Writing, 14*(2), 88–115. https://doi.org/10.1016/j.asw.2009.04.001.

Frey, L. R., Botan, C. H., & Kreps, G. L. (1999). *Investigating communication: An introduction to research methods* (2nd ed.). Needham Heights: Pearson.

Hughes, M. A., & Hayhoe, G. F. (2007). *A research primer for technical communication: Methods, exemplars, and analyses* (2nd ed.). New York: Routledge.

Lauer, J. M., & Asher, J. W. (1988). *Composition research: Empirical designs*. New York: Oxford University Press.

Minnich, M., Kirkpatrick, A. J., Goodman, J. T., Whittaker, A., Helen, S. C., Schoening, A. M., & Khanna, M. M. (2018). Writing across the curriculum: Reliability testing of a standardized rubric. *Journal of Nursing Education, 57*(6), 366–370. http://dx.doi.org.lib-e2.lib.ttu.edu/10.3928/01484834-20180522-08

Nickerson, C., Rapanta, C., & Goby, V. P. (2017). Mobile or not? Assessing the instructional value of mobile learning. *Business and Professional Communication Quarterly, 80*(2), 137–153. https://doi.org/10.1177/2329490616663707

Saxton, E., Belanger, S., & Becker, W. (2012). The Critical Thinking Analytic Rubric (CTAR): Investigating intra-rater and inter-rater reliability of a scoring mechanism for critical thinking performance assessments. *Assessing Writing, 17*(4), 251–270.

Shirotha, F. B. (2016). The effect of indirect written corrective feedback on students' writing accuracy. *Journal on English as a Foreign Language, 6*(2), 97–114.

Stemler, S. E. (2004). A comparison of consensus, consistency, and measurement approaches to estimating interrater reliability. *Practical Assessment, Research & Evaluation, 9*, 4. Retrieved from https://pareonline.net/getvn.asp?v=9&n=4.

Ziliak, S. T., & McCloskey, D. N. (2009). The cult of statistical significance. Joint Statistical Meetings, Washington, DC. Retrieved from https://www.deirdremccloskey.com/docs/jsm.pdf.

Part 4

Workplace Writing Center Professional Development

11 Identity Shifts from an Academic Role

Again, I anticipate that many of the people reading this guide have worked within or are familiar with university writing centers. As I described in Parts 1 and 2, workplace writing center consultations can look very much like those found in university writing centers. Consultants use many of the same approaches and follow similar philosophies in an effort to improve others' writing skills. But one major difference that I've discovered is the way in which writing center consultants need to present themselves.

Identity Shifts

As an undergraduate writing tutor, I was encouraged to think about writing centers as a primarily peer-to-peer resource. My fellow tutors and I were trained to use nondirective methods whenever possible, in order to keep control in the hands of the writer. But we also learned to be flexible, recognizing that some consultations required more direction. For instance, we worked with many multilingual students who wanted more direction on black-and-white issues such as subject-verb agreement. Other times, we worked with students who had never before tackled the genre at hand. So while I knew to be flexible in how direct my instruction was in any given consultation, I also was most pleased when I managed to welcome the writer onto a level playing field, in which they saw me as an ally and not necessarily an expert. I remember an instance where, as a graduate tutor, I worked with an undergraduate student several times over the course of a semester. At the end of the semester, she realized I was not in her same year—and I counted this as a success.

This approach worked well for me throughout graduate school, until I began volunteering at a local high school to help them build their own writing center. After leading a group discussion with ten high school students for half an hour, I invited questions. One student raised his hand and said, "Not really a question, Miss Jess...I just wanted to say that I thought you were a student here". I watched as a few of them mentally reassessed the relationship and experience between us. Clearly, in this situation, I needed to lean into my authority a bit more if I wanted to earn the trust of these students.

This problem emerged in a new form when I first began leading a workplace writing center. At first, I marketed myself as a peer. I emphasized my lack of

DOI: 10.4324/9781003212959-16

knowledge when it came to the technical material at hand, but I promised that I could make writing accessible to anyone that I worked with. This invited many colleagues to underestimate my experience—especially colleagues who had been working there for decades already. To them, my lack of experience in their workplace meant that I wasn't worth their time, that there wasn't much they could learn from me. I once again found myself needing to lean into the authority that I *do* have.

Struggles with power and authority are not new to the writing center community by any means. In "Power and Authority in Peer Tutoring", Peter Carino traces decades of debate over the place of authority in writing centers. Ultimately, he emphasizes the need for fluidity when it comes to establishing trust and authority in writing centers:

> All of this is not to say centers should become authoritative, dictating to students what they should do or not do, but if they are to confront and negotiate the inevitable presence of power and authority, like their tutors, they will need to take responsibility for what they know and do not know.
> (p. 113)

Clearly, I had learned to be comfortable with admitting what I did not know… but I was still uncomfortable with admitting the knowledge and experience that I actually had to offer those seeking my help.

I imagine that other writing center professionals may face similar challenges as they transition to a workplace writing center. Portraying myself as an "expert" was deeply uncomfortable for me for the first year or two on the job. But I found that this assertion of authority was necessary for the success of our writing center. I needed to make my colleagues believe that we had valuable feedback to offer and that our expertise was worth respecting. Not only that, but my colleagues *wanted* access to expertise! They didn't want to hear that I would help them figure something out. They wanted to hear that I knew what I was doing, and that I could help them know what they were doing, too. There are a number of ways that you can establish your writing center's authority without intimidating those who will use your services. Some of these techniques are similar to those used by university writing center directors, while others may be unique to workplace environments. Whether you set out to create a workplace writing center as a solo mission (as I first did) or with a small team, you'll want to incorporate some of these habits into your practice as early as possible.

Additional Challenges

It's not uncommon to see writing lumped into "soft skills" when talking about professional aptitudes. This has always baffled me, as writing is typically the vehicle for professional conclusions or opinions; it's what allows meaning to reach an audience. Perhaps this "soft skills" assumption is what leads many workplaces to think that good writing can be ensured with an afternoon workshop once very couple of years. Or, workplaces depend on overworked and undervalued editors, who are enlisted to "clean up" writing in its final stages.

The actual work done by writing center professionals looks more like teaching or coaching, since it's focused on helping writers to develop their skills and to use them independently. Unfortunately, this means that it's possible for writing center work to become mentally categorized as care work—and care work is frequently undervalued. We see this in exhausting and underpaid careers throughout educational settings, as well as in other care industries. Part of this may be due to the fact that such care work "creates value that is difficult to capture through the market because it has positive spillover effects and involves emotional encouragement, teamwork, and person-specific skills" (Folbre, 2021). Though teamwork and interpersonal skills are esteemed workplace values, it can be "difficult to measure the quality of a service that is tailored to specific people, rather than standardized" (Economic Policy Institute, 2021). Employees outside of a workplace writing center may acknowledge greater ease within writing and revision processes, but it can be easy for them to underestimate the real value and labor that results from one-on-one consultations and group workshops. This is why it's so important to incorporate some of the strategies in Part 3 of this book. But it's even more important to recognize that writing center professionals from underrepresented populations will likely face even greater challenges to their expertise and identity within the workplace.

It's well recognized that women face additional barriers to recognition and advancement within the workforce, especially within the United States. Women with families—whether that means raising children and/or caring for dependent family members—are "encouraged to take accommodations such as going part-time and shifting to internally facing roles", all while continuing to be overworked at the office and at home (Ely & Padavic, 2020). Even though I began my career as a single 20-something (with *no* home obligations), I endured some inappropriate comments from older male colleagues about how they were old enough to be my father. Their default view of me was infantilizing, which made it really difficult to establish rapport within a one-on-one consultation. Furthermore, performing work that could be categorized as "care work" likely underscored my female identity. I can imagine this being an even more difficult situation for LGBTQ+ or gender-nonconforming individuals performing care work, especially outside of a care-based industry. The need to assert oneself as knowledgeable, capable, and worthy of advancement becomes even more vital.

And, of course, race and ethnicity present challenges beyond what I've ever had to face as a white woman. Black women are "promoted more slowly than other groups of employees", "are significantly underrepresented in senior leadership", and "are less likely than women of other races and ethnicities to say their manager advocates for new opportunities for them" (Lean In, 2020, p. 28). Perhaps even worse, Black women "are twice as likely as white women to hear colleagues express surprise at their language skills or other abilities" (p.

28). So not only do my BIPOC colleagues need to work many times as hard to advance in the workplace, they also are likely to have any communication- or writing-based expertise immediately undermined.

All this to say: Establishing ourselves as experts in writing and communication is absolutely necessary for this work. It's the only way to win over colleagues' trust and respect, as well as to earn management's buy-in for new resources, opportunities, and initiatives. Writing centers can serve an important role in helping other employees to learn the language of the workplace and excel; we need to start by advocating for ourselves and making sure that our voices are heard (and valued!), too.

Asserting Your Existing Expertise

Since my earliest days as a writing tutor, I've begun consultations by assuring the client (or tutee) that they know more about the content matter than I do—unless, of course, they were also an English major. This is still a common practice in the writing consultations I lead, but now I spend more time emphasizing my own expertise, too. I introduce myself with my credentials when appropriate, and I have incorporated a number of practices into my daily work life. The first of these practices was to frame and hang my degrees in my office. I wanted people to know that beyond the colorful prints and shelves of writerly-looking books, I knew what I was talking about. I had done the work, and I had expertise to offer.

Publicizing Your Success

More difficult than hanging up my degrees was learning to continuously share my successes with others. I let my manager know whenever I had an article published or when I presented at a conference, and he made sure to publish a brief announcement in our department's newsfeed. Though this took little effort on my part, it was uncomfortable at first. But ultimately, it kept me on my colleagues' radar, reminding them that I was adding value to a resource available for their use. Think about the channels that your own workplace has for communicating news and accomplishments. Seek out mentors and advocates that will help you to celebrate and share even the smallest wins.

Additionally, don't undersell your experience. If you are newer in your career, you know the struggle of applying for an entry-level job that requires (somehow!) two to three years of experience. If you tutored as an undergraduate student, you absolutely have relevant professional experience. There is no rule that says you must have already graduated to count your experience as "professional" or "workplace". Writing centers exist in all kinds of spaces, and experience isn't any less valuable for students concurrently studying for their undergraduate degrees. Even if you *do* have a few years of professional experience under your belt, you can add the years you spent as an undergraduate tutor to this total. Time spent as an undergraduate tutor or writing consultant can be easily overlooked by HR representatives and internal management. It will be up to you to communicate its value and to clearly account for it.

If you're fortunate enough to lead a team within your writing center—no matter how small—be sure to highlight their work and accomplishments, too. Again, use existing channels within your workplace whenever possible. Pay attention to awards for which you can nominate your team members: Many workplaces offer on-the-spot cash awards, recognition of service, or other bonuses. One department I've worked within even had a digital "high five" portal that allowed you to simply share when a colleague had done a great job. I tend to send these to my team members when they've completed particularly difficult consultations or tasks. Even if there's no immediate reward attached to the recognition, it helps to build their credibility. Such recognition can be even more valuable to those who work remotely and have less face time with their colleagues.

A quarterly newsletter is another simple, creative way to acknowledge the work that you (and your team) do. Take cues from other departments or internal communications teams as you think about how to accomplish a similar project. For some of my writing centers, this has been a very basic, three- or four-page PDF that we post to an internal newsfeed. These newsletters frequently include tips and tricks for writing, consultants' recommended reads, advertisement for upcoming workshops, and recaps of our team's recent accomplishments. For instance, a spring newsletter might feature the following:

- Tips for writing an automatic out-of-office response as people take spring break getaways and plan their summer adventures
- Each consultant's favorite book by an Asian-American author, in honor of Asian American and Pacific Islander Heritage Month
- Registration information for an upcoming workshop on writing mid-year reviews
- A recap of the team's experience presenting at the Mid Atlantic Writing Centers Association's spring conference

Writing a newsletter is also a good way for your team to get to know each other a little better, and to share more about yourselves with other colleagues, too.

You can also seek out ways to reward those who use writing center services. When my teams approach a major milestone in the writing center, we create ways for others to celebrate along with us. For instance, when we were about two dozen sessions out from hitting our 1,000th session, we let our department know. We also offered a small prize to whichever colleague ended up in the 1,000th slot. Not only did this encourage people to use the writing center, it allowed people to see how much work we had done in a few short years. When we hit the milestone, we took pictures of the consultant and the writer, then shared this with the internal newsfeed (and, of course, wrote about it in our next newsletter!). With a limited budget and some restrictions around permitted prizes in the workplace, we have generally kept rewards simple—a voucher for free lunch at the onsite cafeteria, a $10 gift card to a local coffee shop, an insulated travel mug, or a nice box of tea. But it's been well worth chipping in for something small in order to generate buzz around our work.

Leveraging Development Opportunities

If you work for a larger organization, chances are that there are already some built-in opportunities for professional development. Some of these may be informal, such as joining leadership groups, while others may be bigger time investments, like attending a weekend-long seminar. Find out where you can access more information about available opportunities, or who you can talk to about sharpening your skill sets. Many workplaces are beginning to think more about how they can invest in their employees and entice them to stay, especially within higher-turnover industries.

Employee resource groups and clubs. One of the lowest-stakes opportunities to develop yourself and network within your workplace is to join employee resource groups or clubs. Names will vary across workplaces, but many have ways for employees to gather and collaborate across department and business lines. Toastmasters International, for example, has chapters in workplaces worldwide. Toastmasters is a great way to strengthen your public speaking skills and to network with peoples you might not otherwise come into regular contact with. Or perhaps your workplace features workgroups or networks that support young professionals, underrepresented groups, working families, or women leaders. Join these! Not only will you learn from others, but you'll be able to share more about the work that you do within your writing center.

In-house trainings and classes. If your workplace is large enough to have a robust Human Resources department, chances are they offer periodic classes on various skills and/or have access to online training portals. Poke around their site or contact a representative directly to find out if there are any relevant to your work. These commitments can be as low as an afternoon workshop focused on a particular skill (e.g., negotiating, team communication). In the past, I have also gotten to understand HR departments better by attending these workshops, and have built partnerships with them to help offer writing-related workshops throughout the year. Your workplace may also bring in trainers from well-established, branded programs (e.g., Dale Carnegie Leadership Series) or may be willing to reimburse your attendance at a nearby offering. Be sure to track your own attendance and to note it in performance reviews as appropriate.

External leadership seminars. It's not uncommon for organizations to sponsor or nominate certain members to attend leadership trainings and conferences, especially if you're working in a major metropolitan area. Your workplace may also have discounted access to resources like the Institute for Management Studies, which offers day-long workshops and networking opportunities for professionals from many different industries. I began attending management seminars well before I reached a management level, thanks largely to my manager's unrelenting advocacy. Even though some of what I learned was not immediately applicable to my situation, it taught me the strategies and outlook I needed to get to the next level.

Tuition reimbursement programs. Another worthwhile inquiry is whether or not you have access to tuition reimbursement through your workplace. In a best-case scenario, you may be able to earn a graduate degree in a relevant area. Alternatively, you could see if taking a few courses or a certification program would be a worthwhile boost to your skill set. You won't know until you ask—and at least asking will demonstrate your willingness to go above and beyond.

Conferences and networking. Even if in-house and on-site resources are limited for you, there are always conferences and professional networking groups to consider. The International Writing Centers Association is a great place to find conferences, meet-ups, and writing groups near you. Just bear in mind that those outside of your writing center may not recognize some of these names. Be your own best advocate and share a recap any time you present at a local conference, join a professional network, or do any other self-driven work to add more value to your role and your writing center.

If you work for a smaller or not-for-profit organization, you'll likely have fewer resources at your disposal. However, it's still worth asking about existing programs and incentives for development. Maybe you can secure at least partial funding for a conference or training fee, or you can arrange for flexibility needed to attend a workday seminar. Perhaps your department can offer some compensation when you purchase books relevant to your discipline. But if you do find yourself with very few options for leadership and development, you can always ask if there's any way that you can help advocate for such benefits.

Summary

Those new to working in a workplace writing center are likely to experience some intrinsic and extrinsic identity challenges—but with the right mindset and strategies, these can be anticipated and overcome. It's important to establish your authority and expertise when you first begin to set up your writing center. Though writing center consultants can still work with their colleagues on a peer-to-peer level, writers are more likely to trust writing center services if consultants communicate their expertise confidently. Earning buy-in and trust from executive stakeholders will also depend on consultants' ability to communicate their intentions and impact. Consultants from underrepresented groups may face additional challenges as they establish their authority; if you are part of a larger writing center team, be sure to advocate for these consultants as well.

Be sure to communicate your success throughout your department and workplace. Share good news from writing center consultants, whether it's related to their personal successes or to a writing center milestone. Utilize existing channels that already reach those in your workplace, and be creative about catching people's attention and staying on their radar.

Set your writing center up for success by being aware of any professional development opportunities. Opportunities both within and beyond your workplace can help consultants strengthen their skills and develop new ones. Participation in accredited leadership programs can also help earn the respect of workplace leaders. The next chapter will dive further into ways to connect specifically with writing center–related professionals internationally, as well as how you can grow your team locally.

References

Carino, P. (2013) Power and authority in peer tutoring. In M. A. Pemberton & J. Kinkead (Eds.), *The center will hold: Critical perspectives on writing center scholarship* (pp. 96–113). Logan: Utah State University Press.

Economic Policy Institute. (2021). *Confronting employer power to address race and gender discrimination and disparities.* [Webinar description]. https://www.epi.org/unequal-power/events/confronting-race-and-gender-disparities-requires-upending-the-employer-employee-power-imbalance/

Ely, R. J., & Padavic, I. (2020). What's really holding women back? *Harvard Business Review.* Retrieved from https://hbr.org/2020/03/whats-really-holding-women-back.

Lean In. (2020). Women in the workplace. Retrieved from https://wiw-report.s3.amazonaws.com/Women_in_the_Workplace_2020.pdf

Folbre, N. (2021). Gender inequality and bargaining in the U.S. labor market. *Economic Policy Institute.* Retrieved from https://www.epi.org/unequalpower/publications/gender-and-bargaining-in-the-u-s-labor-market/

12 Education, Experience, and Professional Development

Writing centers—in a workplace or in any other setting—cannot be successful without the right people leading. No amount of space, funding, publicity, or resources can compete with a team (or an individual) who has the appropriate background and a will to continuously improve. If you are hoping to hire a writing center professional at your own workplace, this chapter will help you to craft accurate job descriptions and recruit the right candidate to lead a center. If you are a writing center professional already, you can use this chapter to think about how you can expand your skillsets and remain connected to related professional networks.

Recruiting Writing Center Candidates

The strategies and techniques described throughout this book all require some fairly specific technical background. It's important to use accurate key words to attract the right kinds of candidates. It can be tempting to use umbrella terms like "English degree" or "sharp editorial eye", but more specificity is needed. Consider using some of the terms and phrases in this section when creating your own job posting.

Education

The level of education that you need from your recruit depends on the outcomes you seek. If you are looking for someone who can coach a small group of writers one-on-one, then you can likely find plenty of qualified candidates without graduate degrees. If you envision a writing center that can quantifiably measure and report its progress internally, contribute research externally, and build out resources for highly technical documents and writers, then you should seek out a candidate with a graduate degree.

Many of the postings for writing center consultants that I've helped to craft have used language such as "B.A. required, graduate degree preferred". Several times throughout this book, I've alluded to the fact that writing center professionals tend to find their way into this work accidentally. For that reason, it's not uncommon to see candidates with an appropriate graduate degree and work experience, but with a less-related undergraduate degree. For candidates with more advanced degrees, I recommend considering undergraduate

DOI: 10.4324/9781003212959-17

concentrations with open-mindedness (and, yes, I may be biased as a former creative writing undergraduate).

The following are areas of study that are absolutely beneficial to a workplace writing center; use these key words in your job postings and look for them in candidate profiles.

Writing Center Studies. Admittedly, finding a candidate with an actual degree or certification related specifically to writing center studies is difficult. This area of expertise is an obvious fit for a workplace writing center position, but it's likely you'll need to branch out to some of the following key terms, instead.

Composition and Rhetoric. This was the course of graduate study recommended to me when I realized I wanted to continue working in writing centers. Those who study composition typically spend time focused on *how* people write or learn to write. Graduate students in composition tracks commonly double as first-year writing faculty, helping new undergraduate students to adapt to university discourse. Composition scholars are generally curious about writing processes and strategies, as well as how to help others write in more compelling or clear ways. Many programs of study combine rhetoric with a composition track, earning the nickname "Comp/Rhet". Unsurprisingly, there are a myriad of definitions for rhetoric—but the bottom line is that rhetoric scholars are concerned with what makes a piece of writing persuasive or impactful. Rhetoric students learn to look at a piece of writing and to carefully consider what moves the writer made to attract an audience or following; likewise, they can recommend ways to make an existing document stronger and more convincing. You may not necessarily think of your workplace's writing as "compelling" or "persuasive", but I would bet that it is. Think about the writing your colleagues produce. Are they convincing consumers to buy a product? Persuading the public to trust a service? Offering advice, evaluation, or regulation in a precarious situation? A rhetorician can help with that.

Technical Writing/Technical Communication. Technical writers and technical communicators are skilled at conveying complex information in a way that makes sense to the intended audience. This field overlaps with rhetoric in its focus on audience, purpose, and understanding. Of course, in a writing center, you're not looking for a technical writer who can simply rewrite or create documents for your colleagues. Be sure to look for some experience in coaching, tutoring, or teaching when considering candidates with a background in technical writing and/or technical communication.

Curriculum and Instruction/Education. Because the goal of a workplace writing center is to help writers improve their skills, those who have studied education are a natural fit. Those who have taught in other settings will likely be comfortable leading and/or designing workshops as well as working one-on-one with writers. Candidates who have specifically studied curriculum and instruction will be well equipped to create educational materials, develop structured learning opportunities, and even create benchmarks for progress. Be sure to look for some technical experience in a writing-related field, however. An education background with concentrations in writing, rhetoric, or composition are a great combination for a workplace writing center. Those who have studied elementary education or have focused exclusively on literature tracks (as opposed to English/writing tracks) may have more difficulty providing critical writing feedback to their colleagues.

TESOL/TESL/TEFL. Three important acronyms to know are TESOL (Teaching English to Speakers of Other Languages), TESL (Teaching English as a Second Language), and TEFL (Teaching English as a Foreign Language). Candidates who have studied in these areas will be particularly adept when it comes to working with multilingual writers. If you have an internationally and linguistically diverse workforce, TESOL/TESL/TEFL experience is useful to have around. There are key differences between each of these areas that are worth considering (Lee, 2021). Both TESOL and TESL backgrounds are related to teaching English to nonnative speakers in native English-speaking countries (e.g., teaching immigrants or exchange students). TEFL, on the other hand, is specifically related to teaching English abroad, in a setting where English is not a native or official language.

Language/Linguistics. Candidates with a background in language or linguistics focus primarily on written words and spoken languages themselves, as opposed to studying writers or the process of writing. Linguists are often focused on the history of words, patterns of speech, or what meaning is embedded in language. It is tangentially related to the other fields listed, and may sometimes cross with other program tracks (e.g., my MA is in Composition, Language, and Rhetoric). When considering candidates with this background, take care to look for some teaching, tutoring, or coaching experience. More than knowledge of language, the individual should be able to help others understand how to successfully use language, especially in written forms.

Experience and Relevant Skills

Each individual workplace will value different combinations of skills and experiences. While it may not be necessary for a workplace writing center leader to have a background in the content at hand, it can certainly be an advantage. But the best candidates will specifically be familiar with writing center scholarship and will feel confident in applying it in your workplace.

Look for the following key phrases in applicants' resumes:

- Writing center tutor
- Writing center administration
- Tutoring director
- Writing center consultant
- Writing center director [or assistant director]
- Workplace writing training
- Teacher/Professor/Adjunct faculty in communication, first-year writing, or other writing-related field
- Teaching/leading workshops

The skillsets that you would specifically like to see in your workplace's writing center will vary according to your particular workplace. The following are excellent key terms to use in your job posting and/or job interview questions.

- Designing instructional materials and resources
- Tutoring individuals one-on-one
- Teaching or tutoring small groups
- Teaching large-group workshops
- Tutoring or teaching remotely/online, particularly synchronously
- Measuring writing performance and progress
- Marketing resources and/or leading targeted campaigns
- Working with diverse populations and/or multilingual writers
- Comfortable working with unfamiliar materials
- Familiarity with writing center theory, pedagogy, and practice

Please take note that these lists are not meant to be comprehensive; finding the right fit in a workplace writing center depends on a variety of factors. For example, while I was looking for local candidates for a workplace writing center in Kuala Lumpur, I was unable to find anyone with writing center-specific experience. This is likely because the study and history of writing centers is much more prevalent in the United States. However, we did find, locally, plenty of candidates with backgrounds in TESOL/TESL/TEFL and who had the cultural familiarity and background necessary to lead this initiative. Having this ideal profile in mind can help an organization list keywords that may attract the right candidates. And in my experience, when the right candidate has found the posting, they are usually excited to hear about the opportunities that can come with working in a nonacademic environment.

Job Posting Template

To get you started, here is a template that you can modify as you begin to build up your workplace writing center team.

The Writing Center is/will be [insert mission statement].

The [position title] is experienced in the one-to-one teaching of writing and aligns consultation practices to the mission and brand of the Writing Center. This position entails working with staff at all levels in one-on-one consultations, as well as developing resources to be used [internally/nationwide/etc]. The [position title] will review documents to provide holistic writing guidance and may offer additional editorial support in some circumstances.

Principle duties will include [mix & match as appropriate]:

- *Conducting one-on-one writing consultations; identifying writing patterns and tailoring instruction for individuals as they work on high-stakes deliverables.*

    Using nondirective, rhetorical approaches to writing instruction that addition-ally incorporate [local/company/government] writing guidance.

- *Evaluating job applicants' writing samples during the hiring process, using a standardized rubric to assess organization, support and analysis, clarity, gram-mar, and proofreading for each sample; providing an overall recommendation based on holistic writing performance.*
- *Monitoring and helping to manage Writing Center online interfaces; promptly interacting with writers to schedule appointments and answer any questions about the Writing Center and its processes.*
- *Providing assistance with creating or updating writing workshops, writing guidance, and additional resources; may assist with additional workshops when needed.*
- *Tracking Writing Center progress using surveys or other research methods on at least a/n [frequency] basis; presenting this supporting data to executive lead-ership at least [frequency].*
- *Designing custom workshops as requested by various business lines, offering at least [frequency/demand].*
- *Developing writing guidance and related resources for the department, with the goal of ensuring consistency across [reports, work products, etc].*
- *Education and experience should include:*
- *A [bachelor's, master's, graduate] degree in English or related field (focus on composition, rhetoric, writing, or TESOL/TESL preferred).*
- *Minimum [#] of years' experience in related field is required[1]*
- *Experience in writing center work or providing writing services*
- *Strong writing and presentation skills*
- *Ability to conduct ethically appropriate qualitative and/or quantitative research*
- *Strong approachability and exceptional ability to work effectively with others; some teaching skills*

Continuing Professional Development

A successful workplace writing center depends on more than just hiring ed-ucated and experienced individuals. It's equally important for the center to maintain up-to-date knowledge of best practices and to forge connections with other experts. With this in mind, an early step should be to establish what types of networks and connections will be beneficial; then determine the necessary executive support and/or funding. Opportunities may include attending or presenting at professional conferences, exploring avenues for re-search and publishing, and networking with regional and/or [inter]national affiliates. Because a workplace writing center can be established in any type of organization or corporation, it is possible that writing center leadership may be otherwise isolated from leaders in this field. To provide colleagues with the best possible services and resources, the writing center team will need to maintain these professional ties.

Connecting in Person

Although at the time of this writing there is no network specifically for workplace writing centers, there are a number of associations and organizations with similar focus. Attending conferences is perhaps the best way to meet colleagues who can help you to improve and think creatively about your work. Even if you don't have the ability to travel for in-person conferences, you can still connect with organizations by seeking membership, subscribing to their publications, and/or following their social media. The following organizations are some that I have personally found helpful in my own workplace writing center journey.

International Writing Centers Association (*writingcenters.org*)

As noted on their website, IWCA "fosters the development of writing center directors, tutors, and staff by sponsoring meetings, publications, and other professional activities; by encouraging scholarship connected to writing center-related fields; and by providing an international forum for writing center concerns". A number of IWCA-led and IWCA-affiliated events are fantastic opportunities to connect with other scholars, including:

- IWCA Annual Conference, hosted in a new location each year
- IWCA Collaborative, hosted annually at the Conference on College Composition & Communication (CCCC, sometimes referred to colloquially as "4Cs" or just "Cs")
- IWCA Summer Institute, which offers opportunities to attend workshops, receive mentoring, connect with colleagues, and work independently on projects

IWCA also has a number of regional affiliates that host their own conferences and events. At the time of this writing, existing international affiliates include: Middle East/North Africa Writing Centers Alliance, Canadian Writing Centres Association, European Writing Center Association, La Red Latino Americana de Centros y Programas de Escritura, and the Global Society of Online Literacy Educators (GSOLE). Currently existing US affiliates include East Central, Colorado and Wyoming Writing Tutors Conference, Mid-Atlantic, Midwest, Northeast, Pacific Northwest, Rocky Mountain, South Central, Southeastern, Northern California, and Southern California. For the most up-to-date information, visit IWCA's website and search for affiliates.

Association for Business Communication (*businesscommunication.org*)

On their site, ABC describes itself as "an international, interdisciplinary organization committed to advancing business communication, research, education, and practice". Recurring ABC events include:

- ABC Annual International Conference, hosted in a new location each year
- ABC Regional Conferences, which include the ABC Europe, Africa, and Middle East Conference; the ABC Southwestern US Conference; and the ABC Western Conference
- Other affiliate and cohosted conferences, including the Corporate Communications International (CCI) Conference and the Global Advances in Business Communication (GABC) Conference

National Conference on Peer Tutoring in Writing (thencptw.org)

NCPTW provides conferences and forums focused on peer tutoring and collaborative learning. As they are committed to undergraduate and graduate involvement, you'll find more academics and students at these conferences than you may at a business communication conference. NCPTW does periodically host joint conferences with IWCA, so involvement in one means you'll likely cross paths with the other!

Online Resources and Publications

One of the most valuable lines of communications in the writing center world is the WCENTER Listserv, which is a mailing list for Writing Center professionals around the world. The International Writing Centers Association's website includes directions for how to subscribe to the mailing list and manage the delivery frequency. IWCA's site also explains how to post to the listserv via a simple email. It should be noted that WCENTER is not an official organization of IWCA, and that IWCA does not moderate or control it. The WCENTER Listserv has become a place where ideas are exchanged, job postings are announced, questions are asked, and experiences and resources are shared.

There are also a number of excellent journals that can help keep your workplace writing center's skills sharp.

The Writing Center Journal (writingcenterjournal.org)

WCJ is the official journal of IWCA. An individual subscription is required to view articles; you can purchase one by visiting iwcamembers.org. You can combine your subscription purchase with an annual IWCA membership, with different rates available for professionals and full-time students.

WLN: A Journal of Writing Center Scholarship (wlnjournal.org)

WLN was originally *Writing Lab Newsletter*, started by Muriel Harris as the first printed newsletter (and lifeline!) for the writing center community.

Though you need a subscription to access the most recent issue at any given time, you can read all of its past issues for free. Subscription procedures are the same as for *WCJ*—you can even pair your subscriptions to *WCJ* and *WLN* for additional savings.

Praxis: A Writing Center Journal (praxisuwc.com)

Praxis is an open-access, peer-reviewed journal published through the University of Texas at Austin's University Writing Center. Its focus includes "articles from writing-center consultants, administrators, and others concerned with issues related to writing-center training, consulting, labor, administration, and initiatives".

The Peer Review (thepeerreview-iwca.org)

Also affiliated with IWCA, *The Peer Review* describes itself as "a fully online, open-access, multimodal scholarly journal that promotes the work of emerging writing center researchers". Work is primarily contributed by university and high school student researchers.

Business and Professional Communication Quarterly (businesscommunication.org/bpcq)

BPCQ is affiliated with the Association for Business Communication; purchased memberships to ABC include a subscription to *BCPQ*. Journal articles often revolve around a featured topic, but generally cover "a variety of theoretical, applied, and practical approaches and perspectives, including program designs and assessment, the impact of technology, global and multicultural issues, qualitative and quantitative research on classroom teaching, and case studies of best practices".

International Journal of Business Communication (businesscommunication.org/ijbc)

IJBC is affiliated with the Association for Business Communication, with a subscription also included in ABC membership. *IJBC* features rigorously researched articles that "contribute to knowledge and theory of business communication as a distinct, multifaceted field approached through the administrative disciplines, the liberal arts, and the social sciences".

This list is not meant to be comprehensive; many excellent, peer-reviewed articles and publications can offer guidance on your path to creating and strengthening your workplace writing center. Any of the journals listed, as well as the sources cited in these books, should provide plenty of jumping-off points for further learning.

Summary

Writing centers are all about collaboration and growth. Even if you are in the early stages of creating or pitching a writing center, it's time to think about the ways that you can find support in others and commit to continuous improvement of your center. Knowing the right key terms to use in job postings, as well as the right educational and career experiences to look for, will help you to recruit a mighty workplace writing center team. And if your writing center begins with just one person (as has happened in my own experience!), there are still many opportunities for that single pioneer to connect with a community of scholars and practitioners. Subscribing to listservs will help your writing center to make relevant contacts, as will attending professional conferences. Reading open-access journals or purchasing subscriptions to other peer-reviewed publications will help your center keep its finger on the pulse of the writing center world. Just as we expect the colleagues we work with to dedicate themselves to their ongoing improvement, we should hold ourselves to the same standards.

Note

1 Experience accumulated as an undergraduate peer tutor should be counted. Most writing center experience is concurrent with educational studies and should not be underestimated.

Reference

Lee, P. (2021). TEFL / TESOL / TESL / CELTA / DELTA – What's the difference? *International TEFL Academy*. Retrieved from www.internationalteflacademy.com/blog/tefl-tesol-tesl-celta-delta-differences

13 Giving Back Local,
Going Global

Throughout this book, I have attempted to demonstrate that workplace writing centers can be versatile, sustainable resources that are well worth the investment. It's clear that providing more writing support in the workplace can have an impact on our colleagues—but for established writing centers, what's the next step?

Writing centers in academic and community spaces have a long history of serving beyond their immediate borders, whether that means providing free online resources to the public or partnering with other groups. Workplace writing centers may find themselves in a particularly privileged position to have a positive impact on their communities. Whether your center is able to contribute time, resources, or expertise, it's worth thinking about ways to expand outreach and promote goodwill both inside of and beyond the workplace.

Classroom and Conference Connections

During my time as a writing center tutor and director in both university and workplace settings, I've had the opportunity to speak with classrooms of undergraduate (and high school) students. Sometimes these connections have happened organically, as when a writing center director reaches out to ask if I'm willing to share more about my job with their undergraduate tutors.

Other times, I have been more proactive. For instance, when the Covid-19 pandemic forced writing centers and classrooms to adapt nearly overnight to all-online environments, I posted to the WCenter listserv to offer my time. I found that many academic writing center directors were eager to have a guest speaker in their classroom, even if only through a video platform. I've been able to supplement existing lesson plans by sharing more about my career journey, providing advice for those interested in pursuing less traditional writing center work, and even leading mini-workshops on a range of topics. Through these connections, I hope to show undergraduate tutors just how applicable their skills are beyond their university writing center; I also hope to offer additional support and real-world examples to the faculty who lead these classrooms. These commitments demand varying levels of time, but for the most part, I've found that even a 30-minute block by video chat can be valuable for students. This is a relatively light lift in the course of a regular workweek, so

DOI: 10.4324/9781003212959-18

I try to make myself available for these requests whenever they arise. Though your workplace may require certain levels of approval to speak on their behalf or during work hours, it's worth establishing a protocol for such instances.

Similarly, I have attended a number of academic writing center conferences as a representative of a workplace writing center. Some years, this has involved presenting on how others can follow this same model; other years, this has meant staffing a booth to recruit local students for internship opportunities. These events not only benefit my own professional development, they allow me to connect with students who may be asking themselves the same kinds of questions about their future careers as I once asked.

Hosting Internships

During most of the years that I've worked as a workplace writing center director, I've been able to host a paid summer internship for an undergraduate student. This is perhaps one of the most direct ways to encourage and excite a new generation of writing center professionals.

There is no shortage of research to support the idea that internships give students an advantage when they begin applying to the workforce—the issue is that the demand for internships way exceeds the supply (Galbraith & Mondal, 2020, p. 3). In my own experience as a creative writing undergraduate, I felt that internship opportunities were particularly sparse for students in the humanities. There seemed to be plenty of internship openings for business students and science majors, but I don't remember hearing about anything in my liberal arts department beyond required student teaching placements. Perhaps I remember this because there truly are fewer internship opportunities for those in the humanities; or, perhaps it's because the opportunities that do exist tend to be unpaid.

Those who work in creative fields are commonly expected to provide free labor in exchange for social capital and alleged exposure (Siebert & Wilson, 2013). This exploitation naturally extends to existing internship opportunities, too. Students in the humanities also end up filling more unpaid internship positions because they have fewer options to work with well-funded hosting organizations (Rothschild & Rothschild, 2020, p. 2). Unpaid internships are problematic for a number of reasons, but most notably because they disadvantage those who cannot afford to work for free—a pattern that ends up perpetuating wealth gaps (Siebert & Wilson, 2013, p. 716). For these reasons—the sparsity of internships for humanities majors as well as the inequity of unpaid internship—I would encourage any workplace writing center to consider offering a paid student internship position.

As well as fairly compensating student workers, it's important to create an internship opportunity that is meaningful. The tasks that interns are assigned should reflect the work that they will be likely to do (or to study) in the next steps of their career. In my own experience, I've typically looked to hire an intern who can help with a current project that I'm working on; but I also take care to ask the intern what their interests are and how the role can help nurture them. In past summers, interns have worked on combinations of the following projects:

- Leading one-on-one writing consultations for their fellow interns
- Hosting resume-writing workshops for their intern cohort
- Creating handout resources on various writing topics
- Designing a marketing campaign for our writing center
- Helping to create updated editions of writing guides
- Developing and analyzing satisfaction surveys for those using services
- Writing and distributing a summer newsletter for the department

Whenever possible, I encourage interns to choose their own path within the internship. We work together to ensure that the experience is relevant, challenging, and interesting to them throughout the summer. And though I've traditionally worked with interns face-to-face, the Covid-19 pandemic also revealed that even a telework internship can be a valuable opportunity.

Volunteering and Local Literacy

If your workplace encourages volunteer opportunities, your team should be well equipped to meet literacy needs in your community! At different periods in my career, I've been able to use my skillset to help beyond the immediate bounds of my workplace. As an undergraduate tutor and as the assistant director of a writing center, I was able to help local high schools found their own student-run writing centers. Beyond (and in tandem with) my postgraduate career, I've been able to work with a local elementary school as part of an already-existing weekly reading program and to mentor a student through the Philadelphia-based nonprofit Mighty Writers. While many reading and literacy programs will accept a wide variety of cleared volunteers, these programs offer the highest benefits when volunteers actually have formal literacy training (Nichols, Kim, & Nichols, 2020).

Interested in forming a new volunteering relationship in your community, rather than giving back through an existing program? Look into the needs of your local library. Writing center and library partnerships are not uncommon—not only do their goals align well, but so do their challenges. For years, both writing centers and libraries have found themselves with tightened budget and with increased pressure to quantify their impact (Epstein & Draxler, 2020, p. 513). Your local library may also have suggestions for other organizations to reach out to, as well.

Though volunteering may be an easier goal for well-established workplace writing centers and writing center teams, it's an important goal for even new centers to consider. If giving back locally to your community is an important value, there are plenty of ways to acknowledge this in your mission and to act on this as you build up your resources.

Global Partnership

One of the most rewarding experiences of my career has been helping Bank Negara Malaysia (Malaysia's central bank) lay the groundwork for a workplace writing center. In March of 2019, I traveled to Kuala Lumpur and spent five days helping Bank Negara plan a writing center using the same model described in this book. While the writing that Bank Negara does is similar to the work that I was used to seeing in regulatory banking, the organization, country itself, and language diversity were all new to me. And yet, within five days (and a lot of advance prepwork), we were able to conduct a few workshops, pilot one-on-one writing consultations, and collect survey feedback from Bank Negara employees. We were met with overwhelming support for the creation of a writing center, which is still in progress at the time of this writing. Though I still meet (virtually) with the team at Bank Negara from time to time, my goal is to guide them through creating an independent, sustainable writing center that will serve their Bank for many years to come.

Though I can share limited other details at this time, this experience has proven to me that this workplace writing center model can be just as helpful halfway around the world. As long as the focus continues to be on helping writers strengthen their skills sustainably, writing centers remain a promising resource for many different environments and locations.

Summary

A workplace writing center is meant to positively impact those with access to it, but there may be more that you can do to positively impact the community beyond your workspace. Tap in to any existing volunteer connections your workplace may have, and see if your team's unique skills can be of use. If no connections exist, find out if your workplace has any policies supporting volunteer efforts more generally, and reach out to your local library or other literacy organizations in your area.

Though hosting a paid student intern over a summer will involve more of a financial commitment from your workplace, it's a great way to create a mutually beneficial opportunity within your day-to-day work. Lower-cost efforts can include volunteering your time to classes of students who would be interested in the type of work that your writing center does.

And finally, joining this new but growing conversation about workplace writing centers may mean that you'll be met with requests for help to start another. Whenever possible, be open to new connections and potential partnerships that will help another organization get the same type of resource off the ground.

References

Epstein, M., & Draxler, B. (2020). Collaborative assessment of an academic library and writing center partnership: Embedded writing and research tutors for first-year students. *College & Research Libraries, 81*(3), 509. https://doi.org/10.5860/crl.81.3.509

Galbraith, D., & Mondal, S. (2020). The potential power of internships and the impact on career preparation. *Research in Higher Education Journal, 38.* Retrieved from https://files.eric.ed.gov/fulltext/EJ1263677.pdf.

Nichols, J. D., Kim, I., & Nichols, G. W. (2020). The effect of parent and community volunteerism on early literacy development. *Educational Review, 72*(4), 411–426. https://doi.org/10.1080/00131911.2018.1530638

Rothschild, P. C., & Rothschild, C. L. (2020). The unpaid internship: Benefits, drawbacks, and legal issues. *Administrative Issues Journal: Connecting Education, Practice, and Research, 10*(2), 1–17. Retrieved from https://files.eric.ed.gov/fulltext/EJ1289868.pdf

Siebert, S., & Wilson, F. (2013). All work and no pay: Consequences of unpaid work in the creative industries. *Work, Employment & Society, 27*(4), 711–721. Retrieved August 29, 2021, from http://www.jstor.org/stable/24442101

14 Conclusion

With increasing shifts toward flexible work arrangements, fast-paced technologies, and globalization of the workforce, workplace writing centers are a timelier resource than ever before. Many workplaces already acknowledge the value of good writing (or at least the pains that come with weak writing), and writing center professionals have exactly the experience and vision necessary to support their needs. My hope is that by starting more conversations between writing center professionals and workplaces looking for writing support, we can create more of these mutually beneficial spaces. Establishing a workplace writing center can help an organization create more efficient processes and more confident writers, as well as open up exciting job opportunities for writing professionals.

Writing centers have, throughout their limited history, evolved and adapted to meet generations of students' changing needs. They have met students where they are and sought to ensure that each student could communicate more confidently, clearly, and effectively. As writing centers have expanded to more varied sites (e.g., high schools, community centers), we've seen more people benefit. It's time for writing centers to stretch one step farther into the workplace. Professionals, I've found, will be just as grateful for the additional support as repeat student visitors are.

Workplace writing centers can particularly benefit new hires as they transition to the workplace from many different professional, generational, and cultural backgrounds. Those first entering their professional careers are especially likely to embrace the support a workplace writing center can offer. More seasoned coworkers are likely to resist writing center services at first, instead asking for more transactional help like copyediting and proofreading. And executive leaders may need to be convinced of the sustainability and benefits that come from hiring full-time writing center staff rather than hiring one-off writing experts to lead occasional workshops. But with proper messaging, it's possible to introduce a workplace writing center that benefits all levels of the organization and that becomes a welcome resource in time.

The messaging around your workplace writing center should be clear and consistent from the very beginning. Ensure leadership's support for the message at hand, and encourage their patience as your center begins to establish itself. You will also need to have conversations about how the writing center

DOI: 10.4324/9781003212959-19

will be used—ideally, this will mean that writers use the service voluntarily, without feeling like their managers are punishing them or looking over their shoulders. Writing centers should be seen as a resource that is allied with writers, helping them reach the next level and taking some of the pain out of the writing and revising processes. By involving writers, managers, and executive leadership to take part in these early conversations, you can begin to earn their trust. You will also learn more about writing relationships within the organization as they currently exist.

In addition to encouraging patience as your workplace writing center gets off the ground, think about how you can begin with smaller pilots and expand services over time. A well-targeted pilot and phased approach can help you to anticipate wider needs, build trust, demonstrate success, and meet eventual demand. Identify leaders who advocate for the writing center, and use them as ambassadors who will help encourage writers to use the service.

It's important to think about how you'll use the resources at your disposal, but it's even more important to think about how you can avoid contradicting existing resources and/or duplicating efforts already in place. Take time to map out what writing support exists within your workplace, and interview staff and managers about what resources they actively use and find helpful. Ensure that writers have access to standardized writing guidance, whether that means promoting and increasing the accessibility of existing guidance, or building a new set of writing guidance entirely. Consider the needs of many different writers as you create these resources, including multilingual writers, those with visual impairments, and those who are less technology-savvy. And if you do have additional writing support in your workplace (e.g., a team of editors), be sure to build a relationship with them so that they understand writing center services as complementary, not competitive.

Writing centers can serve a workplace in a variety of different ways, though I encourage one-on-one consultations as its primary service. Consider how to make these consultations convenient and private for writers. Valuable options can include a physical location with a closing door, an online video chat platform, and consultant prereading to keep consultation length at a minimum. Your writing center may also offer periodic writing workshops, which serve not only to increase a group's writing knowledge but also to keep the writing center's services on your coworkers' radar. As you develop your writing center's services, you will also want to consider whether your writing center will play any role in revision or editorial processes within formal review processes. Whatever you decide, be sure to take a clear and consistent stance, separating the writing center's goals from those of copyediting. You can better promote these services if you develop a consistent and recognizable writing center brand, even if the brand is just a simple logo and consistent language.

Of course, even as you see your writing center begin to make an impact on your workplace, you'll need to think about ways to quantify and communicate this impact to stakeholders. Benchmark surveys, needs assessments, and data log analyses can help you to pinpoint progress in writing populations, as well as help you support any need for expansion or additional funding. You may also choose to conduct pretest/posttest quasi-experiments from time to time in order to look at quality changes in various writing components. As you design ways to measure your writing center's progress and to determine its next direction, think carefully about who you're studying and who will see those results. Respect the writers you work with by ensuring that surveys aren't too frequent, too time-consuming to complete, or likely to expose their identity if you've promised anonymity. Rely on consultation data logs whenever possible, since you can study these data without specifically needing to call on writers for their time and attention. And consider what types of feedback and measurement are truly valued by the stakeholders in your workplace. If you are working with a writing center team, consider issuing internal quarterly and annual reports to help everyone understand your current reach, consultation trends, and milestones to be proud of. Package this or similar information at strategic intervals for leaders in your department or workplace as a whole; be especially mindful of budgeting deadlines or times of year when important decisions are made. It will take time and care to develop research methods that are both ethical and practical for your workplace writing center, but it's well worth the effort. In addition to benefiting your writing center in the long run, you can also help fill gaps in writing center scholarship by sharing your findings.

Be patient as your writing center launches—you generally won't see significant progress in writing quality within the first six months. During this time, you'll need to focus on earning writers' trust and encouraging them to use the service. You may also need to become more comfortable with promoting your own expertise and successes, which can feel counterintuitive to those who have worked in academic writing centers before. Learn about your workplace's communication channels and use them to promote the work that your center does. Be your own best advocate, and do the same for any teammates who work in the writing center with you.

In the same way that you will be encouraging your coworkers to improve their skills, you should keep an eye out for professional development opportunities, too. Investigate whether your workplace offers opportunities to attend leadership programs or specialized seminars—this will not only benefit you and your staff, but can also make your writing center more visible to executive leadership. Be sure to take advantage of opportunities within the wider writing center community, too. Subscribe to listservs, attend professional conferences, and read open-access journals or purchase subscriptions to peer-reviewed publications. It can be easy to feel isolated from the academic writing center community when you're working in a different environment, but by proactively connecting with your writing center colleagues, you can continue to learn from one another. Communicate the importance of these connections and opportunities to your leadership so that you secure the support that you need to attend events or access materials. Hopefully, in time, you will also be able to expand your own writing center team with more professionals as demand grows.

Finally, consider the impact that your writing center can have even beyond the immediate workspace. Many organizations encourage partnerships within the community, and you (and your team) will likely be well equipped to help with literacy-related efforts. Look into whether your workplace will allow you to hire a paid undergraduate intern for a summer or a semester, which can be a mutually beneficial opportunity. Speaking with classes or allowing a student to interview you for a project can also be small but impactful ways to give back to the writing center community without incurring any costs. As more workplace writing centers begin to crop up around the world, you may also find yourself in a good position to offer advice and/or develop partnerships. Pass along opportunity to someone else by helping them to lay the same groundwork that may already be behind you—or lean on each other for support if you find yourself in similar stages of development.

At different stages of your workplace writing center's development, different sections of this guide are likely to be helpful. I encourage you to revisit them often, and to continuously think about how you can improve your writing center's strategy, relationships, and impact. In my own experience, helping workplace writing centers launch has been an extremely rewarding career. I've seen coworkers feel less stressed as they complete reports, celebrated milestone sessions with teams of dedicated consultants, and had many opportunities to connect with writing center professionals doing excellent work in both academic and professional workspaces. When you consider that clear communication is an important skill in just about every job in every industry, there truly are endless opportunities for writing center professionals and workplaces to team up. The challenge now is to start these conversations, encourage open-mindedness, and prove the impact that we're capable of having. We can also encourage undergraduate and graduate tutors to think about workplace writing centers as an emerging career path.

I hope that this guide has made you feel more confident in your own journey to create a workplace writing center. I encourage you to reach out with stories of your progress and success so that we can grow this new community together and continue to learn from one another.

Index

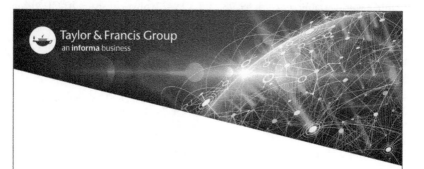

Taylor & Francis eBooks

www.taylorfrancis.com

A single destination for eBooks from Taylor & Francis
with increased functionality and an improved user
experience to meet the needs of our customers.

90,000+ eBooks of award-winning academic content in
Humanities, Social Science, Science, Technology, Engineering,
and Medical written by a global network of editors and authors.

TAYLOR & FRANCIS EBOOKS OFFERS:

A streamlined
experience for
our library
customers

A single point
of discovery
for all of our
eBook content

Improved
search and
discovery of
content at both
book and
chapter level

REQUEST A FREE TRIAL
support@taylorfrancis.com

 Routledge
Taylor & Francis Group

 CRC Press
Taylor & Francis Group